AF747474

"*The Complete Guide to Videogame Performance Directing: Place, Time, Action* is an invaluable resource to learn the magic Tom Keegan delivers in his direction. Now you don't have to be on set to access it — you can literally have it at your fingertips."

– **Troy Baker**, *BAFTA Nominated Actor, Videogame Performance Director*

# The Complete Guide to Videogame Performance Directing

This book teaches the complex, sometimes confounding, and often beautiful art of directing live performance for videogames. Starting from a clear and comprehensive introduction to the nuts and bolts of directing on the motion capture floor and in the voiceover booth, this book dives deeper with concrete examples from the author's 25-year career directing seminal games from the early years to today's blockbusters.

Identifying the Place (*What is the physical environment?*), Time (*What just happened?*), and Action (*What do the characters want?*) of every scene empowers directors with essential tools to dive straight into the subtext, the life below the words. Through step-by-step instructions, this book shows how to make scenes and lines come alive. It offers real-world advice on everything from casting to table reads, rehearsal, and production days. In addition, readers can find valuable advice about self-care and sustaining a long-term career as a performance director.

This book is sure to be an essential resource for directors, actors, voiceover artists, and game developers who want to master videogame performance.

**Tom Keegan** trained as an actor, movement artist, and director, performing in theaters throughout the US and Europe. He worked in animation at Hanna-Barbera Studios and Universal Cartoon Studios before transitioning to videogames in 1998, where he has performance-directed some of the most popular and successful videogames of the last 25 years. His award-winning work includes AAA franchises such as *Battlefield*, *Wolfenstein*, *Call of Duty*, *Resident Evil*, *Need for Speed*, *Dead Rising*, and *Walking Dead: Saints and Sinners*.

He received a BAFTA nomination for his work on *Wolfenstein: The New Colossus*. He is best known for his direction on *Jedi: Fallen Order*, *Jedi: Survivor*, and *Indiana Jones and the Great Circle*. Throughout the year, Tom offers classes in acting and directing through his company, TomK Studios. www.tomkeegan.net

# The Complete Guide to Videogame Performance Directing

## Place, Time, Action

Tom Keegan

CRC Press
Taylor & Francis Group
Boca Raton London New York

CRC Press is an imprint of the
Taylor & Francis Group, an **informa** business

Designed cover image: Catherine Leonardo

First edition published 2026
by CRC Press
2385 NW Executive Center Drive, Suite 320, Boca Raton FL 33431

and by CRC Press
4 Park Square, Milton Park, Abingdon, Oxon, OX14 4RN

*CRC Press is an imprint of Taylor & Francis Group, LLC*

© 2026 Tom Keegan

Reasonable efforts have been made to publish reliable data and information, but the author and publisher cannot assume responsibility for the validity of all materials or the consequences of their use. The authors and publishers have attempted to trace the copyright holders of all material reproduced in this publication and apologize to copyright holders if permission to publish in this form has not been obtained. If any copyright material has not been acknowledged please write and let us know so we may rectify in any future reprint.

Except as permitted under U.S. Copyright Law, no part of this book may be reprinted, reproduced, transmitted, or utilized in any form by any electronic, mechanical, or other means, now known or hereafter invented, including photocopying, microfilming, and recording, or in any information storage or retrieval system, without written permission from the publishers.

For permission to photocopy or use material electronically from this work, access www.copyright.com or contact the Copyright Clearance Center, Inc. (CCC), 222 Rosewood Drive, Danvers, MA 01923, 978-750-8400. For works that are not available on CCC please contact mpkbookspermissions@tandf.co.uk

*Trademark notice*: Product or corporate names may be trademarks or registered trademarks and are used only for identification and explanation without intent to infringe.

ISBN: 9781032906195 (hbk)
ISBN: 9781032914541 (pbk)
ISBN: 9781003558910 (ebk)

DOI: 10.1201/9781003558910

Typeset in Caslon
by codeMantra

Dedicated to all my guides in the theatrical arts: my instructors at Adelphi University; my New York teachers Alec Rubin, Suzanne Shepherd, and later Patsy Rodenburg OBE; my Los Angeles teachers Ned Manderino and, above all, Judith Weston, who helped me put it all together. They represent an unbroken line back to the Stanislavski Method of directing and acting. May this most human of art forms continue to flourish as new technologies present new opportunities and challenges for performance.

# Table of Contents

# Foreword

**By Judith Weston**

When Tom Keegan first came to my workshops, he was already an accomplished director and actor, and yet, he approached every new exercise with enthusiasm, openness, and a fearless imagination. I think my favorite memory of him is from a class in which everyone was to choose a scene from *Hamlet*—and reimagine it in whatever form might clarify its emotional truth for them on a personal and creative level. Tom and his scene partner took the meeting between Prince Hamlet and the Ghost of Hamlet's father—and played it as a zombie movie! The result was both revelatory of a deep emotional truth of the play and consummately entertaining. (Naturally, Tom took the role of the Ghost/zombie. And—no surprise—it was everyone's favorite.)

Tom adopts, before every project, and more naturally and gracefully than anyone I've ever met, the mental outlook of *beginner's mind*. That is, he undertakes every creative task as if it is the most fascinating and meaningful project he has ever encountered. And so, when he told me he was writing a book for directors of videogame performance, I knew it would be a good one. And it is.

This book and the lessons Tom writes about drawn from his experiences apply to performance in any medium. And with the looming threat of technology replacing human actors with digital ones created by artificial intelligence, the art of directing people is more precious than ever. My own firm belief is that although AI may well have legitimate uses in filmmaking and games, it is a tool whose sharp edges are hidden. And that it is now more important than ever for young directors to feel totally confident in their own imaginations before exposing themselves to the seductions of AI. Tom Keegan and I share this point of view and are united in our belief that the most popular stories in any medium are rooted in empathy and the power of the human imagination.

This book is clear and comprehensive. It captures the richness of complex ideas without rendering them lofty or esoteric—and without dumbing them down. It's well-written, friendly, practical, and—dare I say it—inspiring.

Tom's love for actors—and videogames—shines through on every page.

Judith Weston is the author of *Directing Actors 25th Anniversary Edition* and *The Film Director's Intuition.*

# Acknowledgments

This book's journey began during the COVID-19 pandemic, and it has taken over four years for me to complete. I could not have done it without my key supporters. First, I want to thank my business coach, Barb Garrison at InternalGroove.com, who helped me build my career and encouraged me over many years to write a book, even when I was convinced no one reads books anymore. Greg Blake Miller has been an invaluable mentor, writing coach, and editor, with his keen eye for sentence structure, his enthusiasm for story, and his intuitive grasp of this material. I also want to extend my gratitude to my colleagues in the videogame development world, who have given me so much support and so many opportunities to work out these principles. In particular, I want to acknowledge the team at Machinegames, with whom I've worked in one form or another for over 20 years, for their loyalty and spirit of collaboration. My thanks to all the photographers who documented this work and allowed me to use their photographs, especially Sigtor Kildal and Katja Kulenkampff, and Sony/Guerrilla Games, Lucas Arts, Goodbye Kansas, Target 3D, and MachineGames/ZeniMax for their permissions, as well as to all the actors in the photos. Last but certainly not least, my undying gratitude and love go to my family, to my husband Davidson Lloyd, and my daughter Connor Keegan-Lloyd, for their love, support, and belief in me.

Wolfenstein: The New Order: ©2014, ZeniMax Media Inc. All Rights Reserved.

Wolfenstein: The New Colossus: ©2017, ZeniMax Media Inc. All Rights Reserved.

Indiana Jones and the Great Circle: © & ™ 2024 Lucasfilm Ltd. All rights reserved.

KILLZONE™ SHADOW FALL ©2013 - 2024 Sony Interactive Entertainment Europe. Published by Sony Interactive Entertainment Europe. Developed by Guerrilla. KILLZONE is a registered trademark of Sony Interactive Entertainment Europe.

Studio T3D is part of Target3D Ltd.

This book was edited by Greg Blake Miller.

# Introduction: Crying to the Virtual Gods: CD-ROMS

It all started in 1998 at a featureless California office park with kids' educational CD-ROMs. For those of you who don't remember CD-ROMs, let's just say that at one point, they were cutting-edge technology served up on a silver disc. But this is where my videogame directing journey, after years in traditional studios, performance spaces, and theaters, began. It was hard to walk into that sort of setting, across the street from the freeway, for my job interview. I'd become used to the backlot at Universal Cartoon Studios, where I had my own electric golf cart and I could eat lunch at the *Psycho* house and make a quick stop on the *Jurassic Park* ride. Once in a while, I'd see Eddie Murphy riding around on a bicycle. In the commissary, when Spielberg, Katzenberg, and Geffen came through, a hush would fall over the crowd, and people would stop chewing and stare at the gods.

It was also the kind of place where a producer tried to get me fired for keeping him on hold too long.

I'd come to Universal a short time after losing my dream job at Hanna-Barbera in the early days of Cartoon Network. At Hanna-Barbera, I'd been the development assistant, taking pitches and working on the show bibles for *Powerpuff Girls*, *Jonny Bravo*, *Cow and Chicken* and other cool "new wave" animated TV shows. Mr. Hannah and Mr. Barbera, living legends, still came in to work, and the halls of the Jetsons building on Cahuenga Boulevard were lined with original animated cels from the golden era of early TV animation.

But then H-B was sold to Time Warner. We all got fired and the building was sold.

DOI: 10.1201/9781003558910-1

So, I followed my H-B boss to Universal. She was talented, and I enjoyed working with her. The problem was that Universal didn't have a network and the excitement of making shows that would actually go on the air anytime soon. Despite the bragging rights of a studio setting, it felt soulless. And the prospect of getting a promotion or anything on the air was years away. It was the epitome of what is known in the business as "development hell."

One day I dropped a copy of *The Hollywood Reporter* on my desk, and it literally sprang open to the center crease, where a job listing caught my eye:

> *Do you have experience working in children's theatre or animation? Do you have experience with voice acting, comedy or drama? Do you understand how talent is hired and paid? Do you want to create meaningful media for kids?*

Since I'd been to drama school and spent a decade working as an actor, writer, and director, with small success but little-to-no renumeration, I figured, "Sounds like fun. Why not?" I ticked all the boxes and sent in a resume. Shortly after, I found myself in that office park, interviewing for a job as a talent coordinator at the company. I walked the abysmally average hallways—low ceilings, fluorescent lights; you've been there—wondering how I'd gotten here and why. Back on the Universal lot, I had casually dropped to my boss that I was interviewing, hoping maybe a raise or a promotion might come out of it. But nothing like that was on the horizon.

"Don't leave the lot," she warned me. "You'll never get back into television."

But here in the suburbs, away from Hollywood, these offices and rooms were buzzing with energy. Smart, lumpy educators and seriously underdressed programmers and animators sat side by side working out the details of educational games. If I got the job, I would be part of the sound and video group, and they had a fully equipped video stage and voiceover recording studio. The starving artist and fringe performer in me started to get excited. Here was an opportunity and equipment to do something meaningful with my talents and training, and to have fun doing it. There was a growing audience out there for this stuff, educational CD-ROMs, and sales were through the roof. Suddenly, it seemed thrilling to get in on something with a future rather than just a past.

At the end of the day, the hiring manager said, "Just pop in to say hello to one of our managers, Robin. I'm sure Robin will love you."

Robin's office was dimly lit, with a single lamp illuminating a desk full of papers. I sat across from Robin, my best positive friendly face at the ready. It's always important to make a good impression with the "suits."

Robin seemed distracted and tossed out the miserable standard question in an impeccable British accent: "Where do you see yourself in five years?"

*Seriously?*

I gave my usually well-polished, passionate answer.

"I want to make things. I want to make stories that have great characters, to work on projects with a team of other creative people who want to make stuff for kids. Things that are funny, teach good values, and overall make the world a better place. You know, like this place, making educational CD-ROMs. I know how to work a computer, I love technology..."

The suit looked directly at me with those cold capitalist eyes.

*"You. Will. Never. Do. That. Here."*

Robin paused to let those words sink in. I'd been chewed up and spit out before, but never like this, and never in the suburbs.

"If I had to put shit in a box, and call it educational, and get people to buy it, I would. That's not what we're doing here, but you get my drift. I'm hiring someone who can fill that box under my direction. At the end of the day, I'm moving product. That's it."

I gulped and stammered out something like, "OK, well, that's certainly an ... honest perspective. I think I could ... help fill that box."

Two weeks later I had a job offer.

I asked a friend, who was teaching at one of the premiere film schools in the US, if she thought I should risk losing my spot in TV animation for the strange and unknown world of CD-ROMs in the burbs of south L.A. County.

"I think it's going to turn out to be something important," she said.

There are times in life that call you to leap without knowing how or where you will land. But even if you land flat on your ass, taking the risk pays dividends for a lifetime.

Taking that leap into the office park turned out to be the reason I'm here today, the reason I've directed on hundreds of videogame titles from, well, *Barbie Secret Agent* to *Star Wars: Jedi Survivor*, with

*Battlefield, Wolfenstein, Resident Evil, Indiana Jones*, and a BAFTA nomination in between. My road to some of the highest-tech videogames ever produced began with one strange, long-odds bet on the humble CD-ROM. Since I took that leap, life has rewarded me. It turned out that I *was* able to make things with amazing characters. I *did* get to work with some of the most talented people on the planet who use technology to tell stories. I *did* have the opportunity, in some small way, to make the world a better place. One of the joys and responsibilities of directing videogames is that millions of people will engage with your work. It becomes part of their lives. Your adventure becomes *their* adventure.

My job as a videogame performance director has been to make sure that the technological wizardry of these games is endowed with humanity. To ensure that the deeply organic art of human performance turns digital pixels into a dramatic story. And to never forget that at the end of the day, we are, as Robin eloquently put it, moving product.

Ours is an oral tradition. This craft of performance directing cannot be learned from a book, but a book can be a place to be introduced to compelling ideas. A place to find a recipe that you can make your own. A place to hold and reveal secrets and a history of experiences and lessons learned.

Over the course of decades, I've continued to study and refine how human performance can engage, intrigue, and even haunt an audience. This book is a manual of all that I learned from some of the great masters of 20th-century psychological acting. It is a repository of that wisdom and technique adapted for the high-tech world of interactive storytelling. It is the beginning of a conversation that I hope will continue well into future, and my intention is to pass it all on to you. Read the book from the beginning or study the book by trying out the tools in each chapter. It's your turn to take them forward.

# 1
# Beyond the Ones and Zeros

**In This Chapter**

- Introduction to the craft of videogame directing
- A brief history of acting and technology
- Introduction to the Method and Method exercises
- The Meisner Technique
- Acting in videogames: from voiceover to motion capture
- The craft of videogame directing

"The story and the acting," a videogame developer once casually said to me, "exist to hide the 1s and 0s." What the developer was referring to, in tech bro programmer lingo, was the complex mechanics and technology that must seamlessly come together to create the artificial-yet-compelling reality called a videogame. From ancient times, all storytelling has had the same basic purpose. Life is so complicated that humans can only survive by using stories, symbols, and metaphors to convey vast quantities of information.

When I was in high school, the computing machine took up an entire room. To get the machine to do something simple, we created flow charts filled with triangles, squares, and circles, which got translated into punch cards which got fed into the machine. I found the thinking process, which goes something like, "If this, then *x*, if not this, then *y*," incredibly stimulating. The foundational language of computers, based completely on 1s and 0s—essentially, "on" and "off"—somehow spoke to the tech geek in me. But it didn't speak to my creative spirit or to my dreams. That's why we hide the numbers. This sleight-of-hand, turning digits into stories, turning science into myths, turning psychology into

DOI: 10.1201/9781003558910-2

tales, is critical to creating engagement and enabling our brain and our spirit to fully immerse in life itself.

There was a time when videogame makers tried to create this immersion strictly through the power of graphics, sound, and game design. But it soon became clear that deeper engagement demanded a more profound presence, the human presence: actors and their performances. Technology has improved and made this possible. But we are still catching up on the artistic front. Why shouldn't we strive to give videogame performances the same richness that we expect in the best film, theater, and television? In this book, I will set out the fundamentals and philosophy that can encourage and enable deep, impactful, and memorable performances in videogames.

Even with the looming advent of artificial intelligence (AI) threatening the primacy of human performance, the perspective and nuance of a living, breathing, thinking, and feeling human will always be the best and only way to put true soul into the characters in a game. Machines can, at best, only imitate the human experience. Reading this book should give pause to anyone considering replacing human actors with artificial intelligence. Once you understand the profound craft that underlies storytelling through performance, you will celebrate the irreplaceable power and potential of human actors.

And here's the thing about featuring human actors in videogames: It works. Players respond to the human faces, voices, and emotions behind their favorite characters. They become loyal and devoted to these actors. I've seen "unknown" actors gain thousands of fans by getting cast in a single videogame. At signing conventions, fans melt down in front of the person who portrayed their favorite game character because they might have spent months or years in the presence of this character, playing as them or interacting with them.

Directing the actors who create these characters is part of the masterful telling of the story. It is a language and an art form more directly related to theater than film and can be traced back to the Russian master of 20th-century theater, Constantin Stanislavski. We will delve into exactly what this art form and craft entails in each chapter of this book. It's important right now to understand how videogames are made because the process of creating the performances is driven by the unique rules of videogame production. At its heart, the videogame is a collaborative art. It's crazy, it's maddening, it's frustrating, but above all it's fun.

## The Craft of Videogame Directing

I've often described the acting in a game as similar to the icing on a layer cake. And everyone knows that the icing makes the cake. A team spends a certain amount of time building the layers of the player's journey. It's as if they must invent the process anew each time. How will the ingredients come together? How will this cake be new, different, and fresh? It's the icing that shapes the impression of the cake—the *story* of the cake.

After spending months and years working on the layers of a videogame, developers often leave the icing to the last minute. The production process of games is so technology-heavy and complex that the craft and expertise of creating compelling performances are often given short shrift.

Even when there is substantial time, a game developer tasked with directing actors may spend endless hours chasing a performance when, if they had the right tools—oh, say, an experienced performance director—they could make the scenes come together much more efficiently. Here's where the lack of training and craft actually costs time and money. I know of one massively successful franchise where the brilliant creatives have little or no dramatic training but plenty of time and money. They shoot stuff, throw it out, shoot more stuff, maybe get one good scene, rinse and repeat.

When you know the craft of directing, that doesn't happen. The biggest fallacy new game performance directors have is they are there to direct the actors. While superficially that may be valid, the larger reality is that they are there to tell the story through performance. Like the conductor of an orchestra, a good director sets the tone for the production. They balance the work of the fine artists that have been brought together in service to the piece. The director tracks the arc of the story and the way it's affecting the player level by level, scene by scene, beat by beat, line by line. They shape the whole narrative so that the actors can truly engage in the emotional reality of their character's situation. An actor can feel a confident performance director supporting them and giving them permission to fly. The actors are the director's greatest and closest collaborators.

A good director is an ally to their actors and treats them with the greatest respect. Actors are not puppets. Most are like finely tuned racehorses. Once hired, the actor becomes a member of the team. But videogame developers often fail to consider and orient the actor at the level they would for a new hire, relegating them to a daily journeyman brought on to perform a service that can't be done in-house. Yet the service they are performing requires an extremely high level of skill and sensitivity. Throw some material their way and they will turn it into magic. A good director helps the actor make that magic. And an ancient magic it is.

## Acting and Technology: A Brief History

The history of performance styles is driven by the technology used to deliver it. Going way back, Greek theaters were built in an outdoor amphitheater style, and masks and costumes were designed to heighten the voice in those arenas. Often, it was the playwrights who directed and staged the dramas. Shakespeare and Kabuki were developed to entertain rowdy audiences in large open spaces, coordinated by actor/managers. The 19th-century Delsarte acting system of large-studied gestures and poses was perfectly suited to indoor theaters dimly lit by gas lamps. With this style, a new role began to appear: the director who arranged artistic stage pictures.

### *Psychological Realism*

A more truthful style of performance emerged in the late 1880s in theaters lit by electric lamps. At the same time, writers in the West began delving into topics such as marriage, sexuality, mental health, and politics. Playwrights such as Henrik Ibsen, Chekov, Dumas, and Hauptmann began to explore these themes in the theater, and a new approach to acting was needed. The new approach was called "realism," largely developed by the great Russian theater director **Constantin Stanislavski**. Stanislavski's system contrasted the **art of representation** with **the art of experiencing**. The art of representation—thinking that purely *illustrating* the script is the purpose of the acting—is one of the main misconceptions harbored by many visual and technical creatives at the game developer level. What they are really after is the art of *experiencing*.

Moving pictures with sound developed the art of realism even more, and as lenses and sound became more sophisticated, the demands for greater psychological realism in performance grew. At the same time, Americans who had worked with Stanislavski in Russia developed

**The Method**, which came out of the 1930s Group Theatre in New York. A few members went on to start The Actor's Studio, and the Method arguably became the dominant force in acting for the 20th century.

*The Stanislavski Method*

"The purpose of theatre," Stanislavski famously said, "is to bring the life of the soul to the stage." His productions with the Moscow Art Theatre, based on emotional honesty, sense memory, and truthfulness, brought nuance the public had never experienced before. This fit the sensibility of the 20th century and powered the acting behind talking pictures. Lee Strasberg, at the Actors' Studio, later developed this into what became known as "Method acting."

Stanislavski's original Method laid out a comprehensive technique that not only delved into emotional life but also incorporated voice, movement, rhythm, action, and presence. The exercises are profound. They include:

- **Sense Memory**. Sense memory allows the actor to focus their attention on a physical, visual, taste, smell, or sound stimulus. Sensory recall can trigger an actor or any person into powerful states of awareness that are experienced as real. It stimulates the unconscious and gives an actor the ability to go beyond clichés. Directors need to know and understand an actor's process in seeking unplanned discoveries instead of immediate results.
- **Private Moment**. Stanislavski had an exercise which was called "solitude in public." This evolved into the private moment, where an actor is in front of an audience and doing a task as relaxed and naturally as if they were alone. This is an essential skill for an actor, and it's an essential skill for a director to create an atmosphere where an actor can feel free enough to allow their private self out.
- **Affective Memory**. Affective memory allows an actor to recall an emotionally charged experience from the past and allow the feelings to affect their performance in the present. This requires a high degree of skill for a director to maneuver, as the results can veer out of control if they are powerful and

engrossing enough. But this technique can deliver fantastically affecting results.

- **Personal Object**. The actor chooses an object that has an emotional meaning for them. A favorite ring, an animal, or a piece of clothing they might imagine holding or wearing. A prop, set piece, or costume element imbued with a personal resonance gives the character a relationship to their environment and tools.
- **Animals**. A character might be described or based on an animal. The actor may study the animal for qualities of movement or response to create a character that is very different from themselves, yet fully filled with their inner essence expressed in subtle ways through the animal.

Many fine actors and film stars studied Method acting at The Actor's Studio. Unfortunately, the personality quirks of some of these actors have given the Method a bad name. The sensitivity required by the Method became a shorthand for indulgence, mumbling, just "being," or emotional hijinks. The Method is little understood by most today, but its principles are worthy of consideration for all good performances, whether realistic or not. I have studied the Method with one of Strasberg's assistants, Ned Manderino, who put his own spin on it. Manderino's adaptation of Stanislavski and Strasberg, which he called "transpersonal acting," gave actors a broader range of choices in finding their way to the character, encouraging them to reach beyond the self and its experiences into the realms of deep imagination, summoning fantastic images and spiritual sensations. This brought the Method closer to echoing the true breadth and depth of consciousness at work. Manderino was only one of a number of people who developed acting techniques based on Stanislavski's Method. One of the most famous was Sanford Meisner.

### *The Meisner Technique*

Meisner was a contemporary of Strasberg and a member of the Group Theatre. Meisner focused on the action aspects of Stanislavski's system. He wanted actors to be spontaneous and free, not trapped inside themselves or limited by their experiences.

Meisner's basic exercise is a brilliant and deceptively simple one called, the **Word Repetition Game**. Two actors face each other and study the other's face and body. One starts by noticing something physical about the other and makes a statement such as, "You are wearing a red shirt." The other actor repeats the line, "I am wearing a red shirt." The actors at first mechanically ping-pong the phrase back and forth. Meisner taught that this simple exercise got actors listening to each other and communicating without thinking. Later, the repetitions include adding in the actors' point of view and allowing the actors to affect each other. After repeating, "You are wearing a red shirt," the actor might suddenly have an organic impulse to say, "I don't like red shirts."

Meisner's technique very much involves the imagination. His dictum was, "Acting is living truthfully under imaginary circumstances." It doesn't matter whether the actor's dog has died. The actor can imagine any circumstance, *real or not*, and directly related to the acting situation or not. In New York, I studied with Suzanne Shepherd, one of Meisner's protégé's, and she had a tremendous influence on me. Suzanne would always say to me, "just do the doings." She wanted to me to focus, as Meisner did with his students, on having an action to accomplish in the scene and having an effect on the other actor in the scene. Nothing more, no purposefully illustrating emotions, only what came up naturally in fiercely pursuing the goal of the character.

Both "methods" are valuable and important traditions and practices that influence contemporary videogame performance. The predominant values in modern performance are *truth and authenticity*. And for a medium with a production process like videogames, any technique that stimulates and grounds the imagination is useful.

## Acting in Videogames

The earliest videogames had no actors at all. They had pixelated characters with rough animations. The first uses of acting came from voices used to sweeten up the experience of playing a game where the animations were crude, such as in the 1990 *Last Alert*. But within a decade, voice acting grew to be a powerful tool for "hiding the 1s and 0s" and creating immersive experiences for players. In the early 2000s, actors began doing stunts and even performing their own characters in motion capture suits, bringing a new level of subtlety and detail to games. A few years later, the success of the 2009 film *Avatar* introduced body scanning and facial capture technology to the arsenal of performance opportunities humans could bring to the interactive world.

The task of casting and directing the performances in these changing times has fallen on different types of practitioners with various levels of skill. They have ranged from audio directors, writers, and animators to teachers, crew members, and even receptionists. The level of skill—and the type of expertise—is all over the map. The level of quality in performance directing has depended on hiring actors who have the technique and can deliver the goods with a minimum of direction. Because voiceover was the first point of entry for acting into games, historically, audio directors became the prime holders of responsibility for casting and direction.

*Voiceover*

The legacy of voiceover still dominates performance in videogames. Players have come to expect rich voices from voiceover artists who do everything from commercials to trailers to animation. In videogames, acting is sometimes secondary to the quality of the voice. In fact, most of the voice work in games is sprinkled throughout the gameplay and is not in the cinematic scenes. This includes battle chatter, radio calls, and other VO in **multiplayer experiences**. Voice actors who can do multiple characters, as well as healthy screams, battle shouts, and extreme sounds, tend to work over and over and become veritable stars in the field.

The actor is likely to be performing a scene in the voice booth with no scene partner present. They may have no idea how close or far they are to the person they are speaking to in the game. They may have to convincingly perform hundreds if not thousands of random lines, shouts, or screams to a specific character or to no one in particular. They may have to speak a written text in gibberish, such as in the popular franchise *The Sims*, or improvise entire sections of material (Figure 1.1).

**Figure 1.1** Actor Morla Gorrondona performing voiceover for a videogame. (Photo by the author.)

*Motion Capture and Performance Capture*

The other primary vehicle of videogame performance is **motion capture (mocap)**, also called **performance capture (pcap)** when paired with facial and voice recording. Many of you have seen behind-the-scenes clips of how the *Avatar* films were made, so you might be familiar with the process. When first introduced, motion capture, which had originally started out as a medical tracking technology for physical therapy, fostered a sea-change of possibilities for digital character creation.

Mocap and pcap involve actors wearing tight elastic **mocap suits** with reflective **markers** placed at key points and body joints. They may have markers on their fingers, feet, and face (Figure 1.2).

**Figure 1.2** Actor Troy Baker prepares for a day of performance capture for *Indiana Jones and the Great Circle*. (Photo by Sigtor Kildal. Courtesy of Machinegames, ZeniMax, and Lucasfilm.)

Mocap cameras are placed at different levels in the **volume** (the arena where the mocap **capture** takes place.) One of the first things I'm often asked by people unfamiliar with the motion capture world is, "What does the volume look like?"

Picture a large, spare, high-ceilinged space with padded walls and sound dampers in the rafters. The industrial carpet is often overlaid with a grid to aid in marking exactly where objects will be in the game. (Figure 1.3) Motion capture sets are not finely crafted faux castles or space vessels but crude wooden frameworks designed to match the shape, and not much else, of the final rendered object. Cameras are mounted on poles extending outward from the walls. Actors, regardless of how they might appear in the final game, all look like some sort of latex-clad astronaut of the future in their mocap suits and helmet-mounted face cameras. Acting and directing in such a space takes a *lot* of imagination.

**Figure 1.3** The Goodbye Kansas motion capture volume in Stockholm, Sweden. (Photo by Gianni Aliotti, courtesy of Goodbye Kansas Studios.)

Mocap cameras are not optical; they capture no images. Instead, the cameras act as both a light source and a receiver of the reflective light that bounces off the markers on the actors' suits. This is why the sets, as much as possible, can only be frames of rooms and doors. The light to and from the cameras cannot be blocked. Those cameras are carefully calibrated to turn the reflected light points into data. Imagine a screen where an impossible number of dancing dots represent the movement of each marker on the actor's body. Those dots are connected and turned into a moving skeleton, which is eventually fleshed out with a body, costume, and props to become a character. Imagine a planetarium that shows you the night sky, and then connects the stars into constellations and finally fills in a full illustration of Sagittarius or Scorpio (Figure 1.4).

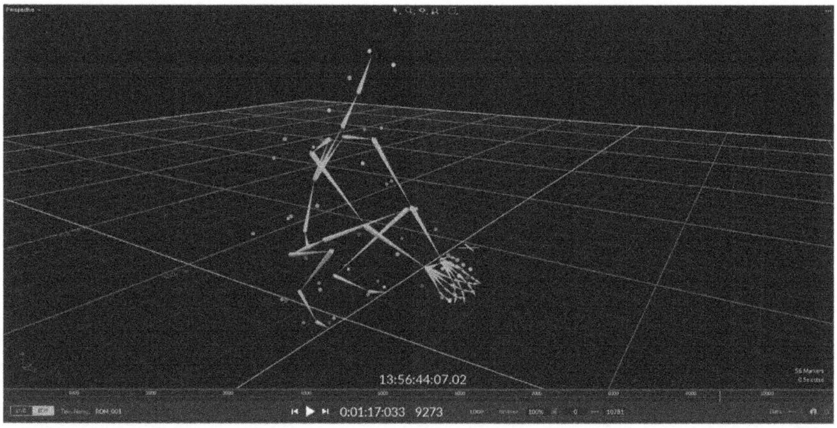


**Figure 1.4** Virtual skeleton of an actor in motion capture. Software: OptiTrack Motive. (Image courtesy of StudioT3D, part of Target3D Ltd.)

Performance-capture actors who are skilled and experienced are in similar demand to top voice actors. The challenges they face are many: They may receive the script at the last moment and have to memorize many pages overnight. They will have to shoot multiple versions of the "same" moment to respond to different player choices. They often have to perform exacting vocal and physical scenes at a high level of competence with a minimum of rehearsal. Scenes need to run from beginning to end with no cuts, as in a play. Some of these demands can really put actors to the test, and directors need to be prepared to help them stay connected to themselves and their material while operating in an extremely challenging environment. I often say I have to create an ensemble of people performing at the level of a Broadway or West End show in one day.

I have often told actors the following to prepare them for the experience:

> *The process of pcap is a stripping away. You will shed your clothes and put on a generic Velcro leotard. Your fine figure and washboard stomach will be covered with reflective markers. Your lovely hair will be hidden under an ugly cap, and your beautiful face and skin will become a dot pattern. Technicians will wire you with equipment including your mic and the large batteries that power it. All you will be left with is your voice, your movement, and your imagination.* (Figure 1.5)

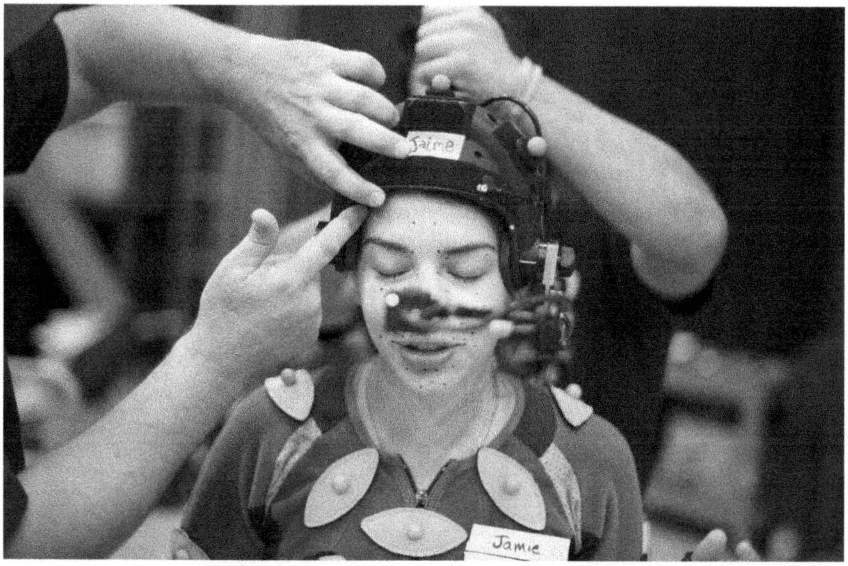

**Figure 1.5** Performance capture actor Jamie Hyder gets her helmet camera adjusted by technicians for the game *Killzone Shadow Fall.* (Courtesy Guerrilla Games. Photo by Katja Kulenkampff.)

For well-established voice actors, the transition to pcap is not always easy. The years spent refining their sound at the mic may have been at the expense of their physical presence, a key aspect of pcap. I've seen voice-acting stars fail miserably at a pcap audition when asked to perform a physical scene on their feet. Many have never been in plays or done acting work outside the booth, and the ones who have drama training may not have acted on their feet in years. Pcap absolutely requires an actor to have full expression not only through voice but also through body and facial movement.

Voice actors may have intensive acting training or none at all. They may have attended a drama school and have acted in plays, films, or TV. Or maybe they're a gifted mimic who can perfectly capture the voices of others. Some VO artists are comedians or singers who have good voices and can improvise. Others have quirky or unusual voices they've used in animation since childhood. Many have huge fan followings in the videogame world. But none of this necessarily makes them right for pcap, which requires, above all, excellence in movement.

Pcap actors usually have been stage actors, stunt people, or have a military background. Depending on their background and training, they may not have an in-depth understanding of acting but are still masters of their craft. Yet when taken into the voiceover booth, they can also fail miserably. Voice acting is precise and technical and for an actor used to swinging from ropes or speaking Shakespeare from a stage, standing behind a mic might muffle their talent. An actor who is able to give a commanding performance both in the booth and the volume is a rare and valuable collaborator.

The exercises developed by the modern masters of theater and film are equally adaptable to games. A knowledge of voice, movement, acting, and the language that highly skilled practitioners of these art forms utilize enhances a game director's value. Usually that language comes out of the performer's training.

### *Actor Training*

Contemporary actors may be trained in a variety of ways or not at all. Some have undergraduate and graduate degrees, with continued professional training throughout their career. Others have mostly on-the-job training. I run across all kinds in my work, and a successful director must have superb communication skills to work with actors at every level.

Training is a life-long necessity for the actor. Acting classes are a vehicle for continual exploration of text and character through scene work. Voice and movement workshops tune the body, the "instrument" through which acting occurs. These classes are the roads to a deep understanding and release of emotion and impulse. Without this understanding, an actor may not have the discipline to sustain the psycho-physical demands of the profession. Like dancers and musicians, most actors go in and out of professional-level classes throughout their careers to refine their work.

### *Imagination: The Heart of Videogame Acting*

For both pcap and voiceover, actors and directors alike need one thing: *a rich imagination*. Film, TV, and even theater actors, to an extent, may rely heavily on the setting or the costume to create the feeling of their reality. The videogame actor needs those details spelled out for them. If the scene calls for the actor to be lumbering in a bulky spacesuit, they'll have nothing like a spacesuit to help them create the awkward gait. If the scene calls for an actor to be trudging through the snow in a polar parka, they'll have no snow, no parka, and nothing cold to make them shiver. All of this is the job of the actor's imagination—and so it becomes the job of the director, too. The performance director must do everything in their power to fill in the details as much as possible for the performer.

There are as many different kinds of directors in voiceover and pcap as there are actors. Many have no training at all in acting or the performing arts, while some are highly skilled. In a sound booth, the voice director may be a trained director. They may also be an engineer who runs the session and coaches the actor. They may be the audio director from the game team who knows what sounds the team needs and what the environments and levels are. The director may be a writer or narrative director whose expertise lies in the scripts, scenes, and lines.

Or they may be a specialized performance director. Hence, this book.

### *Director Training*

When I first began working in videogames as an in-house employee, the company had funding available for professional training. As a voiceover director, working with actors daily, I was longing for inspiration. Having been an actor and dancer who regularly attended professional classes, I wondered what directors did to stay fresh. An internet search turned up the Los Angeles classes of Judith Weston, the author of *Directing Actors* and *The Film Director's Intuition*. I attended her beginning class, "Acting for Directors," and I immediately knew I'd found a major teacher who would have the greatest influence on my career.

Judith's students include Alejandro Iñárritu, Ava DuVernay, Taika Waititi, Steve McQueen, and other major directors on the film scene today. The strength of Judith's training program is her emphasis on directors' understanding of the needs of actors and how to "solve" the scene. Judith taught that there was no right way to do a scene; the key to her approach was to have actors talking and truly listening to each other. The behavior keyword here is "truly." When people truly talk and listen, all their experiences and reasons for speaking are present. She encouraged me, as both a director and an actor to make compelling, unforgettable choices for the reasons characters behave the way they do.

I remember one stirring moment on a rainy West LA evening: The air is heavy with the threat of El Niño. We're sitting in Judith's studio, a small theater in an innocuous strip mall. (You can have the most amazing experiences in Los Angeles strip malls.) A director is presenting a scene she worked on in the "film noir" style. A man and woman are in a bar, chatting the way people do in a bar, with most of the important bits of conversation left out. The actors seem to be talking to each other and listening, but the scene is bland. I've seen this kind of thing over the years, particularly in LA acting classes: Actors talk to each other in such a low tone you can hardly hear them, in the most pedestrian style. This is low-level "film" acting. I hate this; something in me rebels every time I see it. Maybe Judith feels the same way. In any case, she gets up, asks the director if she can make an adjustment, and whispers in the female actor's ear.

They do the scene again.

It's electric, filled with a nameless pain.

This is what I want to study, this is what I want to know: How can one small suggestion change the entire tone of a scene and suddenly make it work? As soon as the scene is over, I raise my hand as if I'm hailing a taxi and shout out, "What did she say? What did she tell you?"

"She told me," the actor says, "to think of myself as damaged goods."

Damaged goods. A woman who's had trauma of some sort. A woman who is a survivor but has a past that's left her broken. Broken ... and dangerous. Even the phrase seems ripped out of a noir script. In that moment I see how a single, unforgettable idea can give a scene life and color. I begin to discover that if I can find choices like that, choices that are so interesting to me that I won't even need notes to remember them, I'll be on to something big.

Over the next 15 years, I take every workshop I can with Judith. And I begin to feel that I'm finally cracking the essence of acting and directing.

### *The Order of Magicians*

The actor's job is to bring the script to life using their imagination, ideas, and experiences. To be an actor is a most wonderful profession: it's an order of misfits, charmers, and empaths who study human behavior and use their imagination to enact scenarios in a heightened reality, opening to the deepest of emotions. Actors are shapeshifters, transforming themselves into any and all manner of humans and other creatures.

In other words, they're a lot like gamers.

Acting is a difficult profession. The common perception is that anything less than starring roles in TV or film means an actor is "aspiring." The facts are very different. According to the Screen Actors Guild, only 7% of working actors make enough to earn a living. They cobble together a variety of jobs, from the occasional TV role to voiceover dubbing to commercials, modeling, and often full-time jobs in other professions that allow them the flexibility to take time off for acting. The actor's dedication is an asset for the director. Remember that every actor you gather in the volume or the booth has made big sacrifices to be there, no matter how they present themselves. The seeming prima donna wants this to work just as much as the overly eager pleaser.

Actors may have started in childhood or later in life. They might discover an interest in doing plays in high school or performing in community productions and go on to professional study. Some are involved in sports or gymnastics and find classes for stunts or creature moves while studying accounting or business. They might have a natural talent for imitation or funny voices, start playing around with making recordings or videos, and take classes with professionals before booking their first jobs. They will do whatever it takes to work professionally at this thing they love.

Once they find an entry into the profession, they must work ceaselessly to refine and expand their talent with a combination of skill and luck to stay competitive. They must constantly audition either live or by recording scenes and sending them to unseen directors and producers. They sacrifice a great deal of comfort and security because nothing means more to them than being given an opportunity to work with others in this profession—a profession that can touch the soul deeply. Whether on the stage, on the set, or in a school, it takes years of training to create a seasoned actor. It's the director's calling to help these dedicated artists thrive. The first step in doing so is discovering the magic of **subtext**, which we will explore in the next chapter.

## References

*Avatar*. Directed by James Cameron, performances by Sam Worthington, Zoe Saldana, Sigourney Weaver, Stephen Lang, and Giovanni Ribisi, 20th Century Fox, 2009.

Burdick, Jacques. "Theater." edited by Joseph L. Gardner, New York: *Newsweek Books*, 1974.

Dower, John, and Pascal Langdale. *Performing for Motion Capture: A Guide for Practitioners*. Methuen Drama, 2022.

Hethmon, Robert H., editor. *Strasberg at the Actors Studio*. The Viking Press, 1965.

*Indiana Jones and the Great Circle*. Developed by MachineGames, published by Bethesda Softworks, 2024. © & ™ 2024 Lucasfilm Ltd. All rights reserved.

*Last Alert*. NEC Avenue, 1990.

Lewis, Robert. *Method—or Madness?* Samuel French, Inc., 1958.

*Killzone Shadow Fall*. Developed by Guerrilla, published by Sony Interactive Entertainment Europe, 2013–2024. ©2013–2024 Sony Interactive Entertainment Europe. "Killzone" is a registered trademark of Sony Interactive Entertainment Europe.

Manderino, Ned. *The Transpersonal Actor: Reinterpreting Stanislavski*. Manderino Books, 1976.

Manderino, Ned. *All about Method Acting*. Manderino Books, 1985.

Manderino, Ned. *Actor as Artist*. Manderino Books, 1991.

Meisner, Sanford, and Dennis Longwell. *On Acting*. Vintage Books, 1987.

Moore, Sonia. *The Stanislavski System: The Professional Training of an Actor*. The Viking Press, 1960.

Richardson, Kalia. "Actors Struggle for Living Wage and Healthcare Amid Hollywood Strike." *Rolling Stone*, 3 Aug 2023.

Schoeffling, Julia Bianco. *The Art and Business of Acting for Video Games*. Nibi Press, 2022.

Stanislavski, Constantin. *Building a Character*. Translated by Elizabeth Reynolds Hapgood, Theatre Arts Books, 1949.

Stanislavski, Constantin. *My Life in Art*. Edited and translated by Jean Benedetti, Routledge, 2008.

Stanislavski, Constantin. *An Actor Prepares*. Translated by Elizabeth Reynolds Hapgood, Theatre Arts Books, 1936.

*The Sims*. Maxis/Electronic Arts, 2000.

Weston, Judith. *Directing Actors: Creating Memorable Performances for Film and Television*. Michael Wiese Productions, 2021.

Weston, Judith. *The Film Director's Intuition: Script Analysis and Rehearsal*. Michael Wiese Productions, 2003.

# 2

# Three Indispensable Tools: Place, Time, Action

**In This Chapter**

- Three indispensable tools
- Place: the power of place
- Time: what just happened?
- Action: what does the character want?

## A Confession

The room was cold and had paper-thin walls. So thin you could practically hear the snow falling outside. I was on my knees, and I was shivering, not only from the cold but also from desperation. What could I possibly do to appease this man standing in front of me, demanding my confession? He held so much power over my future.

I was 16, and I didn't know shit, except for this: my reason for living was the stage. I had done a few plays in community theater. I was president of the Drama Club at my high school. I had no interest in anything besides acting and directing and was itching to get into my professional life as an actor. My goal was to double up on academics so I could get out of upstate New York early and get into a good college that had a drama department. My parents were in the middle of a bitter divorce, and money was tight, meaning there were few family resources for college. I needed to find a place that had good training at a low cost.

A new drama conservatory was starting in the state university system, and I was desperate to get in. State university meant low in-state tuition. The new program at SUNY Purchase had a great

DOI: 10.1201/9781003558910-3

faculty, and the brochures were full of photos of young people in artsy poses in masks, in dance studios, and singing in a choir. It was full of designs and sketches for state-of-the-art facilities to be built—exactly the kind of place I wanted to go. I applied for and was given a time to audition for a slot in the first class at the new school.

The audition consisted of a monologue from a set of pieces the admissions office had provided. I chose a speech from "The Rainmaker," a 1950s drama about a hustler who comes to a small town claiming to be able to make rain. My high school drama teacher coached me, and I rehearsed endlessly in my bedroom. I made my mom and my siblings sit for a command performance in our living room. They loved it. In my own mind, I was completely prepared.

But the day of the audition, I was off-kilter. The three-hour drive to the campus in a raging blizzard was a nightmare. My father was behind the wheel; he was the bad guy in the divorce, and we were barely speaking. We drove down the NY State Thruway in a VW beetle that had no heat and barely functioning windshield wipers. It felt like we might die, but in my mind, not making it to the audition would have been a fate worse than death.

We arrived. The fancy new facilities hadn't been built yet. The auditions were held in a small house in the middle of a large clearing. I sat in the waiting room with my father, nervous as hell. When my name was called, I went into the next room to do my monologue for the head of the department, an esteemed acting teacher from New York City. In the speech, the character tells a story about how he discovered his gift for rainmaking. I knew from the text that he was talking to a woman. That was about all I knew. No problem. The snowstorm was behind me now. I had this nailed.

I looked up at the sky and with grand gestures and a booming voice, transformed myself into a small-town, big-mouthed braggart. I boasted and thundered and railed and charmed and, exhausted, I finished the piece and looked eagerly at my judge.

The man from New York City raised his eyebrows and took a deep breath.

"Did you," he asked, "read the play?"

It was the most obvious question. It sent me into a tailspin. In all my hours of rehearsing and preparation, it had never occurred to me to read the play. "No," I replied, sheepishly.

"OK," he went on, "did you come here with anyone today?"

"My father."

"All right then. Try the speech again, and this time do it as a confession to your father."

It was a brilliant adjustment, but now I was in such a state that I couldn't run with it. Doing the speech as a son's confession of secret greatness would have given it purity and simplicity. But growing up Catholic, I could only imagine a confession as something shameful, something to do with getting a sin off your conscience. I got on my knees and did the monologue again, but all I could think was that my father could probably hear me through those cardboard walls.

I did not get into the school. But what I learned was worth a degree.

Even though I hadn't read the play, I might have salvaged the opportunity if I'd just known what questions to ask. Today, I've worked with thousands of actors, and I'm constantly surprised at how many don't know what to ask before diving into a scene. It's the same with directors. In their excitement to convey their vision to the actor, they don't share the simple facts. This chapter will give you the most important questions that crack the scene and reveal the subtext. Even if you haven't read the play, you can still find out what's going on.

### The Three Tools

When actors and directors are approaching a scene, I advise them to identify three indispensable tools—what I call **PTA: Place, Time, and Action**. For actors, game audition scripts often come without identifying information, and the three tools must be guessed or tracked down. For directors, articulating the obvious is one of the most powerful tools in the bag. Otherwise, it's too easy to get lost in the nuances of a scene, in the demands of the designers from different departments, losing the basic context of the scene and the way the participants will experience it for the first time. Even if you already know the answers, it can help to verbalize the three tools as questions:

1. What is the environment? (Place)
2. What just happened? (Time)
3. What does the character want? (Action)

*Unpacking the PTA*

*As we go down the list, these essentials grow increasingly complex.*

**Place:** What Is the Environment?

Where is the scene set? Are we in a park, a secret laboratory, out in a snowstorm, crossing the desert in a tank? Are there any sounds or extenuating circumstances, such as water, sirens, explosions, or … snakes? Are there physical actions such as fighting a battle, running for cover, or eating a meal? (Rarely in games does anyone eat, piss, or shit, but vomiting seems to happen quite a lot.) Are the characters talking over the sound of a chopper? Environmental storytelling is a big part of a videogame's narrative. Any misalignment between the performance and the environment can break the scene for the player if the characters seem oblivious to the obvious. Characters come to life when they behave in tune with the physical circumstances.

**Time:** What Just Happened?

The narrative moments that precede the start of any scene are among the most critical pieces of information for both actors and directors. A scene is like a hologram that contains everything in the story that came before. Some of the material might be in the script; some of it might need to be filled in with the imagination. And remember that you'll generally be shooting or recording scenes out of order, so an understanding of what just happened to the characters is essential to making sure everything fits together in the end.

Many great scenes and stories begin *in media res* (Latin for "in the midst of things"), where the details and backstory are developed or told later. This is frequently the case in games, where players come upon a scene or are thrust into a scene and then hunt around the environment for the backstory. Nevertheless, the characters must behave and make choices according to everything that has happened so far—or what reasonably *might* have happened, considering what we know about the characters and their world. Their behavior and relationships are a key part of what makes this form of storytelling so engaging.

Games present unique challenges to understanding the previous moment. There might be multiple possibilities based on what a player has chosen to do or experience—and, of course, it's impossible for a director to know what a player will do. But the director still needs to understand what *might* have happened and make choices for the scene that work for every possibility. So, if I'm a director just getting started with this sort of project, the mind-bending question that arises is: *How do I know what just happened when there's no way of really knowing what just happened?*

Of course, the first and most obvious idea is to ask someone. Ask the writer, ask the narrative director, ask the game designer. For the most part, in a game script, there will be no information about what just happened because most likely it will be gameplay, and gameplay isn't usually reflected in the narrative script. So, some digging around might be in order. I've heard horror stories about performance directors who reject any input at all from the game team. But for a performance director, the game team is your invaluable ally. So is your imagination—over time, you can train your mind to come up with workable answers to the "What just happened?" question when even the developers themselves don't know.

A **previous moment** can be the last time these characters were together, or any key moment from the past that is relevant to the relationship. Another way of looking at the previous moment is by asking, "Why now?" Did something just change that forced the squad on a new mission? Is a character's secret in danger of being discovered? Was a battle won or lost? Did we encounter a character who needs something from us?

Previous moments set the stage and emotional temperature for the scene. A line reading can change entirely according to a previous moment. Picture this scenario: A game actor gets a script emailed to them. They come upon a line of dialogue on the spreadsheet: *I need a phone*. No context, except perhaps the filename. In the crush to get thousands of lines recorded and delivered, no one had time to give context. Yet, the previous moment may have been as different as having witnessed a horrible accident to having just been given a top-secret mission and told to collect supplies.

### **Action:** What Does the Character Want?

Actions are a profoundly useful element in the performance director's toolkit. But what do we mean by action? Pure and simple, an action is something an actor can *do*. An action is sometimes called an objective.

It is what the character wants. There are two levels of action: physical local actions and psychological subtextual actions.

A physical action can be a simple, local action, such as, "Shawn comes into the room and opens the safe." The local action is, "to get the safe open." Sometimes an action is a long-term, physical objective covering several scenes: "To go behind enemy lines, locate the safe house, and pick up our agent." Each scene may have sub-physical objectives along the way as things get complicated: to wipe out the guards, to solve the puzzle code on the lock, and to disarm the traps at the door.

The subtextual action is much deeper. It powers the physical action and gives the character psychological fuel. Take Batman, for example. What is Batman's physical action overall? To clean up Gotham City. His psychological action? Here are a few possibilities: to avenge his parents' death at the hands of the darker elements of Gotham City, to show his dead parents the man he has become, to get his parents' approval (even if in his mind), to make up for not having been able to prevent their deaths at the time.

Notice that in each of these possibilities, I have included the word "to," followed by a verb. *An action for a character is best expressed as a verb.* Why verbs? Because a verb is something an actor can DO. The best action is called a playable action because an actor can focus on doing that during the scene. Doing something keeps the actor from "emoting" or illustrating emotions. It's much more authentic for an actor to *experience* an emotion that naturally arises in pursuit of their objective, based on whether they are getting what they want or not, than to *pretend* to have one. Actions are the most powerful tool in acting.

We will go much deeper into actions in subsequent chapters. But know this: by making Place, Time, and Action the essence of your director's toolkit, all the levels and nuances of the craft will eventually become available to you.

## Reference

N. Richard Nash. *The Rainmaker*. Samuel French, 1954. https://en.wikipedia.org/wiki/N._Richard_Nash

# 3
# Finding Spine and Subtext

**In This Chapter**

- Illustrating vs. experiencing
- The subtext below the words
- The spine of a character
- The three questions as essential tools
- The spine of the character
- Finding the spine
- Unspoken secrets

In our discussion of PTA, place, time, and action, action is by far the most complex element. As a young actor and director, I used to dutifully select actions for my scene work. As homework, it was pure drudgery because I held a common beginner's misunderstanding of action. I would go through my scripts, identifying action verbs for every line based on the most superficial aspects of a scene. "To walk across the stage … to explain myself to her … to pour myself some water … to take a drink …" These verbs were merely restating the character's movements (**blocking**) and adding nothing juicy or insightful to the scene. Contrast these bland words with something I might choose for a character today: "To put her at ease before I get her to accept a suicide mission. To paint his idealism as a weakness. To see if she has any useful intel." There's danger and hidden motives in these phrases which might feel exciting for an actor to play. And while it still might feel like obligatory homework, once you understand how to select great actions you will see how powerful they are as director's tools.

DOI: 10.1201/9781003558910-4

### The Subtext: The Life Below the Words

The difference in depth between an actor who is merely *illustrating* a character's life event and an actor who is *experiencing* the life event is vast. Illustrated moments and words trap both the director and the actor in clichés and boring choices that, rather than illuminate, obscure the meaning of the scene. In the David Lynch film *Mulholland Drive,* Betty, the lead character, is an actor. With a big audition coming up, she's practicing her scene at home with her roommate. Betty is trying to bring the scene alive, but the words come off stale. In the audition scene, the character seems to be threatening her father's best friend. Wielding a kitchen knife, she says "I'll kill you ... I hate you ... I hate us both." Betty, the actress, plays the scene with domineering anger and rage, screwing her face up, and then breaks into laughter at the absurdity of her audition script.

However, when Betty goes before the casting director for the audition, a handsome, older Hollywood actor who plays the scene with her turns it into a seduction. Naomi Watts, as Betty, plays the scene brilliantly and goes with the moment. The seduction suddenly turns into a sexual game: "I'll kill you" takes on a whole new meaning, as a kind of dare. Just as the actors are about to kiss, she whispers, "I hate you ... I hate us both," as she is clearly in the thrall of the opening moments of an illicit affair with her father's bestie. In this case, "I hate you" means "I want this so bad even though I know it's not going to lead anywhere good." She is playing the truth of the encounter between two characters and allowing the words to serve that truth. When the life beneath the words is rich, the words take on new and engaging meanings.

Subtext is the surging river of life below the words: the history, the wants, and the conflict between the characters. The words are the boulders, rocks, and stepping stones for the actors to navigate. They are the tools for the characters to affect each other. In an emotional moment, they spill out and tumble on the current of feeling. The words are important, but what is more important are the moments. A conversation is moments. Think of most of the memorable scenes you have watched: you remember the goals and what the character is doing more often than the words.

Imagine it's a nice day. You are sitting at a sidewalk café with a drink. You lean back in your chair, and behind your cool sunglasses you are covertly observing a scene at a table nearby. People watching. A neatly dressed woman, about 25, is sitting at the table. With her is a similarly aged man in a tattered leather jacket and unwashed hair. They appear to be waiting for someone and don't speak. In a few moments, a well-dressed older woman approaches the table and goes right to the younger woman, who rises to greet her.

"Hello mother."

Awkward pause.

"Robert was able to make it."

"Hello dear," says the woman, kissing her. "Hello Robert."

She sits down without looking at Robert.

If this was a script, here would be the dialogue:

```
INT. CAFE FLEUR

   ROBERT and GABBY are sitting at a table.
   Gabby rises to greet CHARLOTTE.
                    GABBY
   Hello mother. Robert was able to make it.
                  CHARLOTTE
          Hello dear. Hello Robert.
```

The simplest of scripts, yet a whole story exists that is not reflected in the words. *The story exists in the subtext.* Who are these people? A young couple? Brother and sister? Why are they there? To announce they are getting married? To get money from the mother? The reverse? To confront a family issue? Are they intelligence operatives, meeting to exchange information or to surveil a target? Are they being watched?

All these different scenarios are examples of what we call the subtext. The life below the words. The scene you just read could literally play in thousands of different ways. How would we choose which subtext to apply? For starters, *let the **facts of the scene** and the characters lead the way.*

### The Spine: The Driving Desires

Instead of prescribing a correct way to play the scene, subtext allows juicy possibilities in endless permutations. While narrative and action written into the script can provide clues to the subtext, there are other ways to find the life below the words. Each character has something unique and very important they want more than anything else right now. By identifying what each character wants the most, the psychological space where these different desires meet and clash is in the subtext. These driving desires are often called a super objective or a **spine**, and it's important to know how to find them.

A spine is the essential quality, action, or driving motivation of a character. It is the one thing that will not change during the course of the story. *The facts of the character are a good jumping off point for beginning to develop the spine.* It's important, and often surprisingly difficult, to look at "Just the facts, ma'am," especially if the development team has gone through numerous iterations of a character. Different teams within a studio are usually developing different facets of a character, such as costume, hair, body, voice, movement quality, or abilities. Any clash in those departments and the qualities of a character can start to drift. You might find your lithe, athletic character is suddenly saddled with an enormous brass belt and can never sit or lie down in a certain position. Articulating the spine of the character to other team members can avoid these kinds of misaligned decisions. Also, as you go deeper into subtext and more ideas are generated by your actors or your team, you will need to go back to the facts to keep the circumstances of the character and scene clear and simple.

My own process goes like this: No matter how much I know about a character, I start by making a short list of the facts from the script and from any materials the team has given me. I start with the basics: age, gender identification, race, nationality, profession, outstanding physical characteristics, special powers, etc. I call these known facts. Now, the character has aspects and a personality way beyond these facts, but the first instinct of the viewer is to make assumptions based on these facts. "Oh, that's their son." "She's older, probably the boss." "They look rich, must be royalty." Later, when my directing preparation increases in complexity, I will want to return to these essential facts to keep my eye on the simple truths of the scene.

Once you've made a list of the facts, it's time to ask, "What might a person, with the facts of a character like this, *want* at this point in their life and in this story?" The wants of people in their 20s versus people in their 40s or 70s are vastly different on certain levels, and deeply the same on other levels. People from different cultures and civilizations also have varying wants and desires based on what is available to them and what they've been brought up to value.

The life of a character outside a story can be imaginative and richly telling. For example, many US soldiers in the Iraq and Afghanistan conflicts of the mid-2000s enlisted for the post-service benefits, such as college. Many ended up staying in for multiple tours to take advantage of the large signing bonuses that were being dangled to keep them fighting these unpopular wars. Not all were looking for military careers or were prospective students—many were farmers, schoolteachers, workers in a Midwestern Dairy Queen. Soldiers fight in conflicts for many different reasons. Of course, many fine people in the military have a deeply held sense of service and patriotism for their country and cause. So deep, they are willing to give their life for it. Others might be in it for adventure, or to gain discipline or a community. For a director, considering such facts allows some compelling, and often surprising, choices about the different members of a squad. The unit commander might be from a military family and have a need to uphold their family legacy. A working-class squad member might be looking for a solid foundation, a leg up in life. The gunner might be escaping a dysfunctional family or a bad reputation in a small town and might even be looking to end their life in a blaze of shame or glory. As you get to know the characters better, you start to see the shape of what we call the spine of the character.

To go deeper, a director might ask, "What intuitively calls to *me* about this character? What would be fun or interesting to explore? What would I want or how would I behave under similar circumstances?" And of course, because it's a videogame and is being made by a team: "What have I been told by the writers or developers about these characters and their purpose in the story?" Having noted all these factors, brainstorm and write down possible subtextual actions for each character. This also helps to separate and individualize the cast right at the outset. *Each character must have their own unique spine.*

Let's look at some examples of brainstorming a character's spine: What would a 38-year-old male tank commander on a dangerous mission in the Middle East want at this moment in life? Some ideas might be: *To prove himself. To go home a hero. To make it through alive so he can return to his wife and children. To overcome the shame of a divorce.* What would a 60-year-old female wizard charged with protecting a village want when the ground opens up and demons come pouring out? While there aren't many studies on mature female wizards, we *could* ask what a powerful woman late in her career would want when faced with a crisis in the community. She might want to pull the community together to make a united front. She might want to model boldness and poise in the face of terror. She might want to face this as a final test of her mettle. At the end of the story, the question can be asked, "Did they get what they want, or didn't they?" The spine is the guiding light for all the choices made about the character, or the POV of the character, no matter what is happening *to* them. The spine informs choices when they're in danger on a battlefield, and the very same spine informs choices when they're back on their home planet and in love.

*To make the world safe for my unborn children. To uncover my hidden past. To revenge the genocide of my people.* Notice the use of the word "To" in most of the ideas presented here. Notice how it gives the character a purpose filled with drive and action—a "playable" action for an actor, with a compelling verb after the "to."

Playable means different things in different contexts. In a scene, a playable action has a verifiable result. They get what they want, or they don't. A character wants to affect another character or group of characters, and they get the result or they don't. In terms of a spine, which involves the entire story, the action may be playable or more of a psychological motivation that doesn't reveal its result until the end.

Every human has similar characteristics in their existence. We are born and will die. We create relationships, we engage in tasks, we have desires, wants, and needs. Now, of course, we may have a character outside of these limitations in a game, right? Characters that are immortal or non-human. Yet, since our audience is human, we look at their wants as a character through a human lens.

Finding the basic facts about a character and asking, "What might somebody with that set of circumstances want?" points us to where we do our research, especially for characters that have experiences vastly different from our own. The internet offers a vast library of articles, blog posts, and videos of what motivates different types of people from different backgrounds. Talking to people about their thoughts and feelings and listening deeply to their answers can tell us a lot about them as a character. Travel to other countries. Walk around a city. Watch, listen, take notes, interact, ask questions, *think*—you'll find yourself gradually assembling an internal dictionary of humanity in its vast diversity. When you talk to people, you'll unearth amazing stories.

When I was preparing *Battlefield 5: Nordlys*, a war story about the resistance in Nazi occupied Norway, an opportunity presented itself to take a week-long trip to Oslo and beyond. "Research," I thought. I had long wanted to see the fjords and they didn't disappoint, but toward the end of the trip I still hadn't done any research. After a long hike in a mountain village near Vassar, I stumbled into a museum gift shop. Tired, hungry and scratched up from the arduous climb, I started leafing through a book when an older fellow greeted me. He was a volunteer working at the museum, and a certified local. I started asking him if he'd been alive during the war, but he was born shortly after. Still, I asked: Did he know anything about the resistance during the war? He lit up and began telling me that this very town was the center of the resistance. In fact, his good friend's father was a resistance leader, and the friend had a small museum at his house. Would I like him to drive me over to see it right now? I stumbled onto a treasure trove of radios hidden in drop containers, fake papers, and photos of civilian women training with machine guns. He told me more about the perspective of the local Norwegians than any book could. This experience proved the value of personal connection and research.

Discovering the subtext in theme and character is a process of exploration leading to a rich bank of choices and ideas. There is no end to the levels of exploration. But keep them as subtext.

Recently, I was in a workshop with some very fine writers, working through the first draft of a script for a new franchise that hadn't even come to market yet. We were discussing outrageous ideas for some key characters, ideas that could be mind-blowing to the player. Like actors, we decided to have "secret" actions, intentions, and ideas that juice us up. Ideas we don't articulate on the surface or write, but which the team has deemed guiding-star principals. But later I was disappointed to find these ideas turned into lines of dialogue.

Why do I recommend keeping these ideas "secret?" Sometimes encouraging writers to explore subtext goes weirdly, even hilariously wrong ... because they forget that it's *sub*text. It's not the first time I've given subtextual notes and ideas to a writer, only to be disconcerted to find they've turned them into spoken lines. The **subtextual idea**, "Maybe she knows she's going to kill her hostage from the beginning and getting him to offer up info in exchange for his life is just a game," gets turned into a line: "This was all just a game. I was always going to kill you." Or "This character has never known love" becomes "I have never known love." This kind of on-the-surface (and on-the-nose) approach waters down the power of subtext. *Subtext is most powerful as unspoken secrets or cloaked feelings and intentions.* The friction between text and subtext helps immerse the player deeper into the lives of the characters.

## References

*Battlefield 5: Nordlys*. Developed by EA DICE, Electronic Arts, 2018.
*Mulholland Drive*. Directed by David Lynch, performances by Naomi Watts, Laura Harring, and Justin Theroux, Universal Pictures, 2001.

# 4
# Analyzing the Script

**In This Chapter**

- How to divide a script into dramatic units
- Script analysis: the director's creative homework
- Connecting to the themes in the script
- Steps of script analysis
- The emotional event of the scene
- Finding playable actions

Here's a story, maybe true, maybe not, but helpful for our purposes: It's 1947, the original production of *A Streetcar Named Desire* is about to hit Broadway. Tennessee Williams is ready for a crowning moment, Marlen Brando is primed for a star turn as the brutal Stanley Kowalski, and Jessica Tandy is set to bring life to the tragic Blanche DuBois. And a little-known actor has prepared to play a single scene, as a doctor who whisks Blanche off to an asylum.

"What," the actor is asked, "is *A Streetcar Named Desire* about?

"Well," he says, "it's about a doctor who whisks this lady off ..."

The thing about this story is that the actor, from an actor's point of view, is not wrong.

An actor sees the entire scene from the point of view of their character. A director, on the other hand, can't afford to have such a narrow focus. The director must understand every character throughout the whole story. Directors keep their eye on how all the levels, scenes, and beats drive the action and the story toward the climax and conclusion.

How should we dig into the story? How should we ask the right questions and find the foundations of the drama and characters that guide directorial choices? A study of human behavior helps a director understand and build a reality for players that feels exciting, fresh, and

DOI: 10.1201/9781003558910-5

true. When we research and strive to understand the real-life behavior of people and creatures (including ourselves), we gain the tools to put more creativity and spontaneity into our directorial choices.

This spontaneity, in turn, transforms the cinematics, encounters, events, and gameplay into rich narratives that truly engage players. But for spontaneity to arise, the director must know and understand the bones of the story—the driving force that structures the drama.

As we know, games often have features that might frustrate a storyteller accustomed to traditional linear narrative. How can a grounded and nuanced performance arise from a story that will be co-written by players and the choices they make? What tools can a director use to sculpt performances within this medium? Interactive scripts are, quite frankly, weird. First of all, they're usually delivered to you as spreadsheets. No context, no descriptions, and massive plot holes.

How is a performance director to approach this strange beast?

### Interactive Scripts

Take it from me, it's no fun as a new director working on a project to be handed an enormous spreadsheet with the dialogue of the whole game listed in running order, sortable by character, line number, or scene. Especially when the title is something like *Projectlithium/dialogue/final/ready_to_record/notfinal/DONOTUSE*. Sometimes the script actually does look very much like a narrative film script. Or a linear document that describes all the gameplay with small bits of scenes tucked here and there. But even if a game script looks like a traditional script, massive amounts of connecting material will be missing. Material that is "in-game" won't usually be written like a film script because the action will be entirely player-driven. This includes:

- **Events**. Sequences where player choice determines the next line.
- **Open-World Walk-and-Talks**. Dialogue that goes over passages where players are moving from place to place.
- **Battle Sequences**. Radio calls, battle shouts, and barks (Figure 4.1).

| FUNCTION | LINE | FROM | TO |
|---|---|---|---|
| Tossing grenade | Fire in the hole | Player | Teammates |
| Player shoots teammate | "I'm friendly." "Cease fire!" | Player | Everyone |
| Player melees teammate | "What the hell?!" | Player | Everyone |
| Player throws grenade near teammate | "Fire in the hole!" | Player | Everyone |
| Player in trouble | "Taking Fire" "I'm pinned down." | Player | Everyone |
| Nearby teammate sniped | "Enemy sniper!" | Player | Teammates |
| Player honks horn X times within Y timeframe | "Get in!" "Hop in" | Player | Teammates |
| Nearby teammate killed by tank | "Enemy armor!" | Player | Teammates |
| Player destroys tank | "Armor disabled!" | Player | Teammates |
| Player kills X number of teammates | "Report to your commanding officer for court martial!" | System | Player |
| Player hits teammate with tank fire | "Rogue armor!" | Player | Everyone |
| Player runs over teammate in vehicle | "Watch where you're driving soldier!" | Player | Everyone |
| Player sticks vehicle | "It's gonna blow!" | Player | Teammates |
| Assault soldier disables X tanks | "If we had more soldiers like you, this war would be over." | System | Player |
| Player sticks enemy soldier with sticky grenade | "Nice stick!" | System | Local Player |
| Enemy grabs team's flag | "Flag taken!" | System | Teammates |
| Team grabs enemy's flag | "Enemy flag taken!" | System | Teammates |
| Plays when a teammate pick ups the enemy flag that was dropped | "We have the enemy flag" | System | Teammates |
| Plays when a teammate pick ups the enemy flag that was dropped | "We have stolen the Axis Flag." (have taken...) | System | Teammates |
| Plays when a teammate pick ups the enemy flag that was dropped | "We have stolen the Allied Flag." (have taken the..) | System | Teammates |
| Any flag is dropped | "Flag dropped" | System | Teammates |
| Allies drop the flag | "Axis flag dropped" | System | Teammates |
| Axis drop the flag | "Allied flag dropped" | System | Teammates |
| Enemy drops flag | "The enemy dropped our flag." | System | Teammates |
| Your team dropped the flag | "We dropped the enemy flag." | System | Teammates |
| Generic Flag return message | "Flag returned | System | Teammates |
| Flag returned to enemy base | "The enemy flag has been returned." | System | Teammates |
| Friendly flag return | "We returned our flag." We returned our flag; Defend it" | System | Teammates |
| Your team grabs flag | "We have the flag. Defend the flag carrier." | System | Teammates |
| Plays when the Axis take the flag (to the Allied soliders) | "The Axis have our flag; return it!" | System | Teammates |
| Plays when the Allied take the flag (to the Axis soliders) | "The Allied have our flag; return it!" | System | Teammates |
| All-purpose Flag captured | "Flag captured" | System | Teammates |
| Enemy capture | "The enemy captured our flag." | System | Teammates |
| Allies capture Axis flag | "Axis flag captured" | System | Everyone |
| Axis captures Allied flag | "Allied flag captured" | System | Everyone |
| Friendly capture | "We captured the enemy flag" | System | Teammates |
| Plays when the flag is returned to enemy base | "Enemy flag returned!" | System | Teammates |
| Plays when an enemy takes the flag. | "The enemy has our flag! Return it!" | System | Teammates |
| Plays when the flag is returned to enemy base (If you are Allied) | "Axis flag returned to base." | System | Everyone |
| Plays when the flag is returned to enemy base (If you are Axis) | "Allied flag returned to base." | System | Broadcast |
| Plays when an enemy grabs your dropped flag | "The enemy has our flag." | System | Teammates |
| Enemy flag-carrier is killed | "Enemy flag dropped." | System | Teammates |
| Friendly flag-carrier is killed | "Our flag has been dropped!" | System | Teammates |
| Team returns to base with flag, but flag is in enemy possession | "Return our flag!" | System | Teammates |
| Plays when player acquires the flag. | "You got the flag! RUN!!" | System | Player |
| Plays to nearby allies of flag carrier. | "Cover me! I've got the flag!" | Player | Player |
| Plays when allied player in proximity to flag carrier and only when near | "You're almost home!" | Player | Player |
| Plays when a nearby player passes near friendly flag carrier. | "I've got your back, hurry home soldier." | Player | Player |

**Figure 4.1** Example of a multiplayer script in spreadsheet form.

No matter the format, divide the script into units that can be analyzed and further subdivided. Start by considering:

- **The Entire Script**. The whole script contains themes and a journey of some kind that has a beginning, a middle, and an end.
- **Acts**. A game script may fit into the traditional **three-act structure** of prologue, complication, and resolution, or even the **five-act structure** of prologue, conflict, rising action, falling action, and **denouement**.
- **Levels**. Game units in a particular location or environment, or that have a specific kind of fighting style, weaponry, characters, etc.
- **Scenes**. A group of characters in one place performing a series of actions with a unifying through-line.
- **Events**. Interactive moments that require player choices in action and/or dialogue.
- **Beats**. A unit of action in a scene where a particular topic is discussed. A beat can change when a new topic is introduced

or the emotional tone of the scene shifts. (Sometimes, the word beat is used by a writer to indicate a pause or silence in the dialogue, but this is different. Here, we are talking about a beat as a unit of a scene.)

- **Battles.** Large or small high-action activities utilizing character voiceover and efforts.

### Script Analysis

Script analysis gives you a deep understanding of the material—the foundation of all the work that will follow. Doing script analysis is similar to turning the soil in a garden. Like a gardener who knows the soil's composition and quirks, a director who has analyzed the script knows how to choose the seeds that will flourish in this particular soil and season. You can pivot at the moment, knowing which creative choices fit the script and which are weeds that clutter the story.

When we talk about "doing the **homework**" as a director, we are essentially talking about script analysis. My years of studying acting taught me much about script analysis, and my teacher Judith Weston helped me take this art to a much higher level. In *Directing Actors*, Judith recommends that even writer-directors, who created a script and know every word in it, perform a script analysis as if they were directing a piece written by someone else. This is truly great advice. No matter how much a director already knows about a story, they must put all that aside and look at it fresh. Why? *Because they must understand the perspective of a first-time viewer, or in the case of videogames, player.*

In each scene, examine the situation from the POV of every single character, no matter how big or small. It's tempting to skip the small characters, but then what does a director say to an actor in a small role who says, "What am I doing here?" As Stanislavsky himself said, "There are no small roles, only small actors."

Each role must be examined from a non-judgmental perspective beyond good and evil. Nothing makes a scene stronger than viewing it as a clash of titans—equal energies fully committed to their action. This is why it is nearly impossible for an actor to direct a piece they are also performing in. Their natural inclination will be to view everything from the POV of their character. Only a very disciplined actor-director with a lot of support has a shot at doing justice to a piece under those circumstances.

Script analysis is at the heart of directing. Discovering a subtext for the script is a fun process—and there is no one way to do it. Some directors focus on story beats, plot, and action. Others free-associate with personal connections to imagery in the script, look at paintings, or listen to evocative music. It can be done alone or with others, sitting at a table, or standing and moving while saying lines aloud. I often act out scenes in the privacy of my room, a one-person show of all the voices. While "working through the body," I am flooded with insights about the subtext of a scene that wouldn't occur to me intellectually.

Because designing games takes a long time, often the end is not written when the first scenes are shot. In this way, a game is like a TV series. Each level is an episode, and the entire game is similar to a season. Even in an open-world game, without a linear story, there are fixed narrative points and junctures, gates through which the player must pass regardless of how far they have wandered.

### *Steps of Script Analysis*

What follows is a series of steps you can explore to dig into the subtext. Again, there is no right and no wrong. Use these steps as a jumping-off point for your own dive into the subtext. Keep it fun and intuitive.

### *Step One: Read the Script and Make Notes*

My first notes on a script are the questions I jot down as I read. The player or viewer is likely to have the same question at the same point. I note holes in the writing and things I don't understand. I make a list of topics to research. It's also important to note top-line ideas about the characters or the story; after this first reading, I'll never again be so completely in the mindset of the player, seeing and hearing all of this for the first time. I also ask the developers for a synopsis of the gameplay because a narrative game script always contains massive holes and won't make sense without an understanding of what happens between the cinematics.

### *Step Two: Ask Yourself, "What Is This Game About?" and "What Is This Game About for Me?"*

I scribble these ideas in a notebook, stream-of-consciousness. What of these characters' situations resembles my own life? What is of interest to me about this piece? Why do I want to direct it, and what do I have to offer to this story?

Here's some examples of my own ideas on games I've directed. *Battlefield 3*, while on the surface a story about a terrorist plot, for me is woven through with themes about authority and the need to go beyond authority when the truth demands it. *Mirror's Edge* is about a futuristic corporation that seeks to put chips in the brains of civilians and eventually control the population, but in my mind, it's about how deeply the legacy of long-lost family ties shapes a life for years to come. The plot of *Wolfenstein 2: The New Colossus* is the retaking of the United States from Nazi rule. My personal idea is that it's about the loves and losses of people dedicated to a cause and the shifting power dynamics of life on a submarine. These become the guideposts for deeper choices in each act, level, scene, and beat.

To flesh these themes out, I give myself plenty of permission to nudge, noodle, and poke around the topics of the game. What are the prevalent ideas on the surface? What do the environments and characters say about the human condition today? History seems to repeat itself in spirals: same dilemmas, different causes, different stakes. What are the main emotional concerns of the characters? If I were in that very situation, what would be my concerns? *Mirror's Edge* mirrored my personal struggles to resolve some family complications at the time of my birth that left deep emotional scars. My connection to my own trauma helped me to normalize the dramatic situation of the characters and find the unexpected moments for emotions to break through. For *Wolfenstein*, I connected to the situation of the lead characters, a couple who were expecting twins. As a parent to a young child, I recognized the deep commitment to making a better world for one's children coupled with the absolute terror that any mistake might get me killed, leaving them orphans.

Anything mentioned in a script is a candidate for a theme. Sometimes, the authors are quite clear—almost too clear—about the themes of the script, but there is no end to what's below the surface. A writer articulates a particular theme, but another theme clearly emerges from the actions and motivations of the characters, one that may be entirely unconscious to the writer. I normally find that writers and developers are excited to be shown these subconscious themes by actors and directors. It allows them permission to discover and own what they are really feeling the script is about, despite what the executives or the marketplace may deem "commercially viable."

During this exploration of themes, I don't censor myself at all. I allow everything that occurs to me to come to the surface, and I jot it down in a notebook. Most games are franchises, and your work on them may go on for years. I have found that these early brainstorms are the very things I turn to again and again for inspiration.

### *Step Three: Focus on the Characters*

After my inquiry into the themes of the game and my own connections to them, I come up with candidates for the spine of each character. I write down a few succinct ideas, usually (though not always) in the active "to" form followed by a verb and some description:

- To come to terms with my complicated family legacy.
- To rid the world of Nazis for the sake of my unborn children.
- To wake the government up to the dangers of rogue terrorists.

Judith Weston also encouraged us to consider choices for the spine that would *never* be right. So if I'm struggling to find the character's spine, I list things that I imagine they would *never* want or do. I have found that this approach always illuminates what the character's true spine might be.

This early work on a spine is very useful for casting, which often comes long before the final scripts are written.

### *Step Four: Progress to Scene Work*

Now that you know the spines of the characters, which will remain constant during the game (unless, at some point, it becomes necessary to revisit), it's time to focus on how those spines function in individual scenes. Scenes are the building blocks of the narrative and cinematics, whether captured in mocap or voiceover. Scenes often set the context for the in-game lines, the spoken lines that happen during gameplay and that comprise most of the dialogue in a game.

Here's a good exercise as you start to work on a scene: Read the stage directions as mere suggestions and clues to the subtext, then cross them out so they don't limit the possibilities of the scene. While these stage directions may eventually be honored and strictly adhered to in the end, a good practitioner takes care to avoid illustrating them and instead finds the true, lived experience of these directions (if they survive to the shoot day).

This exercise—which intends no disrespect to the writer—is especially important for your early work on the script. When writers put a script on paper, they are essentially transcribing their imagination. The written directions and responses of the characters to each other are the *writer's* idea of how the scene should go, and the audience is the *reader*. This stage of the script has tremendous value and very likely may end up being exactly the way the scene will be played. For gameplay reasons, there may be physical and emotional actions that are required for the game to move forward.

But in the process of turning page into scene, a new set of imaginative players—the actors and the director—have to deal with different realities, and this may change the nature of those writerly stage directions and parentheticals. The manner and timing of the directions in the script must earn their worth. By removing the author's ideas of how a scene plays, directors can open themselves up to other possibilities of how it *might* play. This exercise is even more critical for a game director who has either written the piece or is incredibly familiar with it.

As a director, you might recoil in horror at this idea. Why dare even consider such a reckless exercise? What if all the directions and demands—all the developer's needs from various departments—were stripped away? What would you be left with? A pile of dialogue? But think: What *else* might you see? What might you have missed that would be obvious to a first-time viewer? What might you discover? What is life in this situation asking from you as a director? In the answers to these questions lies the opportunity to see things in a whole new and necessary light. Even if you end up going back to the original stage directions, you will have found fresh ideas about the life below the words (Figure 4.2).

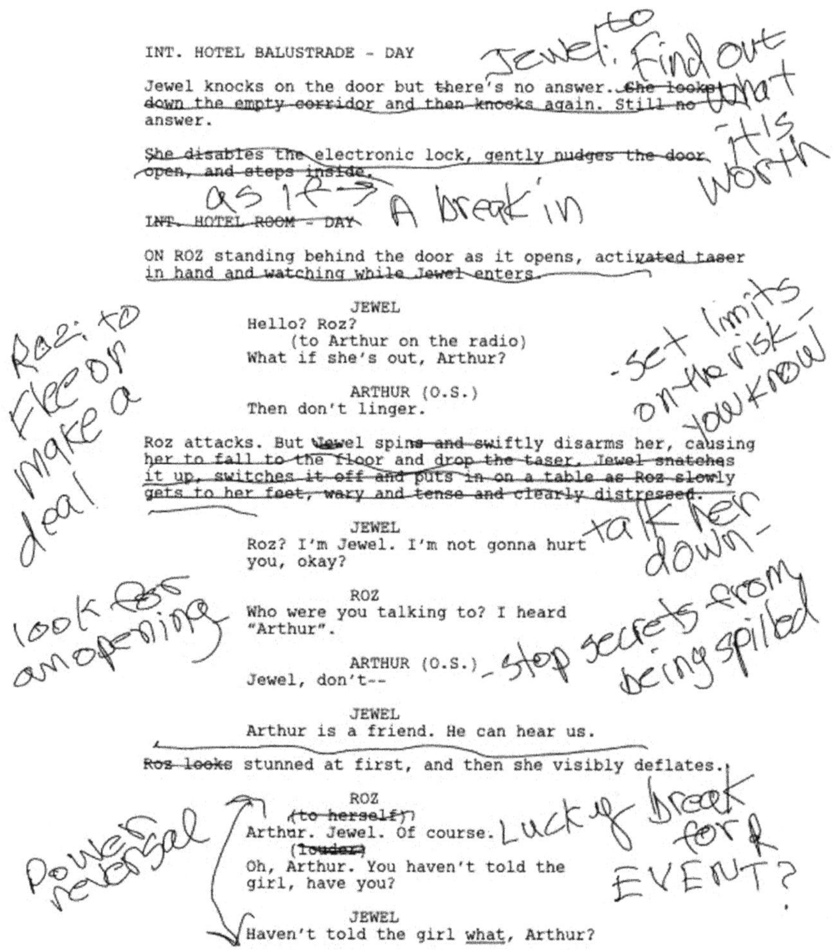
INT. HOTEL BALUSTRADE - DAY

Jewel knocks on the door but there's no answer. She looks down the empty corridor and then knocks again. Still no answer.

She disables the electronic lock, gently nudges the door open, and steps inside.

INT. HOTEL ROOM - DAY

ON ROZ standing behind the door as it opens, activated taser in hand and watching while Jewel enters.

JEWEL
Hello? Roz?
(to Arthur on the radio)
What if she's out, Arthur?

ARTHUR (O.S.)
Then don't linger.

Roz attacks. But Jewel spins and swiftly disarms her, causing her to fall to the floor and drop the taser. Jewel snatches it up, switches it off and puts in on a table as Roz slowly gets to her feet, wary and tense and clearly distressed.

JEWEL
Roz? I'm Jewel. I'm not gonna hurt you, okay?

ROZ
Who were you talking to? I heard "Arthur".

ARTHUR (O.S.)
Jewel, don't--

JEWEL
Arthur is a friend. He can hear us.

Roz looks stunned at first, and then she visibly deflates.

ROZ
(to herself)
Arthur. Jewel. Of course.
(louder)
Oh, Arthur. You haven't told the girl, have you?

JEWEL
Haven't told the girl what, Arthur?



**Figure 4.2** A hand-notated script analysis with the stage directions crossed out.

Analyze each scene based on its purpose, the actions of the characters, and the life beneath the words. Only then will you brainstorm blocking and performance ideas that arise from the subtext.

*Step Five: Identify the Purpose and the Event*

Understanding the purpose of the scene is critical to staying on course with the story. At the top level, what does this scene do for the story? Does it introduce a key character? Set up the main dilemma or task of the characters? Give the player a look at the backstory of a relationship?

Introduce a new plot twist or complication? Tie up a relationship or loose end?

In addition to pushing forward the narrative of a story, scenes have a purpose in the gameplay—pointing out danger, setting up a quest, creating teams, dropping hints, or taunting the player into a fight. Scenes are also about letting the story breathe after intense action, giving the gamer a rest and time to absorb deeper, more thematic content.

Remember PTA? Place, Time, Action? Once the physical circumstances and previous moments have been examined and taken into account, the meat of the scene revolves around the action. A good scene has something at stake, and there is a change of some kind during the scene. There are characters or teams of characters—including the player—who each have wants and desires.

One strong key to script analysis is to find *the change moment* in the scene. It's the moment something shifts, the moment the reason for the scene is revealed. Judith Weston calls it an **emotional event**, and I like thinking of it that way. It's not just when the task is completed or the information is passed on. It's the moment the implication of the exchange is felt, the moment when a character or a team accomplishes the "effect" they want to have on the opposing team or character. Generally, the strength of a character's action is measured by the effect it has on another character. A good scene has characters in conflict, not in simplistic "perky agreement." For the scene to have an event, there has to be a moment where the conflict gets resolved or moves to a new level in some way. I like to call it a "win" even if the stakes are very low.

A working scene always has some major or minor conflict or friction between the characters, or teams of characters. Conflict is not always negative. Two people doing a three-legged race, with one leg tied together, may have the same goal, but even the slightest difference in rhythm or tempo will produce a "conflict." In the same way, characters might have the same task and the same domestic action, but they should never have the same psychological action. Otherwise, the scene will have no dynamics.

When I look for the central event in a scene, and when I investigate what actions I might imagine for the characters, I look to give each character an action that would put them in a pairing that will cause sparks, even if tiny ones. But you can't just randomly assign conflicting actions to cause sparks. The actions still have to fit into the spine of the character and the purpose of the scene.

The event must move the story forward. Game scripts are so long that sometimes, scenes get unconsciously repeated, even though the dialogue is different. If the captain is always chewing out the private, by the third time, it's boring and repetitive. What is different about it this time? If the event changes, if something different happens from the conflict, the story moves forward. Once the director can identify the central event and the moment the conflict comes to a resolution, the scene becomes dynamic.

*Step Six: Find Playable Actions*

Remember that all of this preparation is just examining the possibilities of the scene. Whenever a director is dealing with subtext, there are intuitive processes at work. Having answered the PTA—Place, Time, Action—and having identified the event of the scene, I look for each character's "wants" below the level of dialogue. I break each scene into beats where a topic is discussed or an exchange unfolds. I look for each character's desires on a more and more granular level, from scene to beat to line. I keep asking two essential questions: What does the character want, and what effect is one character trying to have on another? How can I verbalize that as playable action verbs? The best playable actions *create a response in another character.* When an actor puts his focus on stimulating a response from another character, their focus shifts from self to scene.

Actions are sometimes expressed as something that has an observable result. For a *physical* action, a result is usually more observable than for a subtextual action. The safe is either open or it isn't. The squad member has been rescued or they haven't. For a *subtextual* action, the proof may or may not be observable. Batman will never be able to see the look of pride on his parents' faces except in his imagination. But if a character's subtextual action is, for example, "to charm," they can look for that glint in the eye of their scene partner, or a change in vocal tone. The scene partner's response is an indication that the action is working.

Salespeople know this strategy very well. I have often asked an actor in a scene, "is your scene partner making you feel such and such? Are they arousing any kind of feeling and ideas in you?" If not, then the action isn't working and a new one should be explored.

A strong action is exciting for an actor to play. It's intriguing and puts some fire in their belly. A weak action is pedestrian, bland, and on the surface. "To ask" is very weak. "To interrogate" is much stronger. A strong action is simply more playable. I always try to make sure the language that I use to verbalize the action is engaging for the actor. If it's not engaging, I'll change it on the spot.

When I've identified a great action for one character, I look for something juicy for the other character to counter with. Sometimes my choices are on the nose, academic, the obvious. Sometimes they're inspired. They pop into my head and instantly I know they will be sterling and fun to play for the actor. Sometimes if I'm stumped, I'll put down a boring, obvious action as a placeholder. Then as I work through all the beats of the scene, coming up with actions, I usually get an insight into what could be a good replacement for the placeholder. Or, I play the opposite game, brainstorming things it would never be, and then look at the opposite of those. I won't rest until I get something that is either so good I can't forget it, or so much fun that I can't wait to get with my actors and try it out.

But here's the big caveat: I have to be willing to let all this go once I get in front of the actors. As a director, I have to remember, all the time, that ultimately, *the actor will have their own secret actions to play, their own secret images of what the scene means to them.* It's my job to help them find a spark that fits the moment, but in the end, the spark is theirs. For directors, the homework exists only to discover the possibilities of the scene so that when rehearsal and performance take place, you can spontaneously work with what is happening at the moment. It's a fluid and organic process.

**BOX 4.1: Case Study on Subtext**

In *Mirror's Edge: Catalyst*, the main character, Faith, is a runner. Set in a futuristic society where corporations run everything, including the lifestyle enhancement chips they've planted in people's heads, a runner is a parkour expert who stays off the grid. They deliver messages, gather intel, and nick items of value for paying customers. Faith is in hock to Dogen, a yakuza type, and when she works off her debt to him, she can claim something very precious to her: a drawing from her dead mother that Dogen has in his possession.

In one scene, Dogen needs Faith to complete a final mission for him: a daunting break-in to the family apartment of a corporate overlord. But Faith is at a low point, as she has just suffered several personal losses and is a wanted criminal. She enters the room full of rage and loss, seeking to defy Dogen by turning down the mission and demanding he recognize her feelings. So the actions are, "get Faith to take a dangerous mission" vs. "defy Dogen." The stage is set for a confrontation.

According to the script, it's Faith who is full of emotion, with Dogen playing it cool. In take after take, we just can't seem to make the scene work. The emotional content is lopsided; the actors are too polarized. I take a break and do what I usually do when scenes aren't working. I go back to the facts. Dogen's world is closing down and he needs her to do something for him so he can get a win. Faith is in an emotional state. On the surface, she wants to get free of Dogen's control and get the drawing. Underneath, she has suffered personal losses and needs an anchor to rage against or cling to.

Suddenly, I get an insight based on her opening action: "To defy Dogen." What if he uses that to manipulate her? In the script, he tries to talk her into the mission with no luck, and then calls her out on the fact she once would do anything, and now she's just broken. I ask the actor playing Dogen to work at keeping her off balance, blowing up at her when she least expects it but when it feels right to him. And I ask him to end the scene by calling her out in the tenderest way, talking to her as if he were a nurturing father. Even though these are not his actual words, it's as if he's telling his daughter, *It's all right, darling, you were once brave but it's OK if now you're just a loser. You're obviously just broken.*

The adjustment has an immediate effect. You can practically see the hairs rising on the back of Faith's neck as she tells him, essentially, *You're wrong. I'm not broken. You'll see.*

## References

*Battlefield 3.* Developed by DICE, Electronic Arts, 2011.
*Mirror's Edge Catalyst.* Developed by DICE, Electronic Arts, 2016.
Weston, Judith. *Directing Actors: Creating Memorable Performances for Film and Television.* Michael Wiese Productions, 2021.
Williams, Tennessee. *A Streetcar Named Desire.* New Directions, 1947.
*Wolfenstein II: The New Colossus.* Machine Games/Bethesda Softworks, 2017.

# 5
# Working with Actors

**In This Chapter**

- Speaking actor language
- Giving adjustments
- Directors' tools for actors
- Improvisation
- Creating authentic emotional moments

I recently ran into an actor I knew, loved, and had worked with numerous times. She shared with me that she had booked a starring role on the revival of a beloved sitcom with well-established characters. "The problem is," she confided, "I'm the new person on the show, so I'm treading carefully. The director who works on most episodes is constantly giving me line readings and telling me how to play every moment." She looked glum. "I don't know where I am. I feel like I've lost touch with my instincts. I don't feel like I can try anything because I fear it will be wrong."

She paused for a moment and then confessed:

"I'm starting to hate being on the show."

None of us want to become *that* director.

Many people labor under a misconception of what it takes to direct performers. I myself recall telling a friend in the early days, "It's the easiest job in the world!!" Just getting decent-sounding actors to do the lines and barks was a triumph. But times have changed. Cinematics are more filmic than ever. Stories are sophisticated, and millions of new and old players are demanding high-quality performances. Performances that aren't cheesy and melodramatic. Performances that are authentic and riveting.

DOI: 10.1201/9781003558910-6

Just because you have an idea in your mind of how something should go doesn't make you a director. Neither does being able to record many lines per hour or force-marching stunt performers through all the scenes on the schedule. You may be sitting in the director's chair, but are you practicing the art?

It all starts with communication (Figure 5.1).

**Figure 5.1** The author and actor Dave Fennoy discuss the script before a recording session. (Photo by Katja Kulenkampff.)

## Speaking Actor Language

Once a director has a basket of ideas and choices for the subtext of a scene, the next step is to experiment in the laboratory of the studio on living actors. Without becoming the dictatorial line-reading-puppet-master, how do you engage actors in your vision as collaborators? What kind of directorial techniques work best, and how do you apply them in a good way?

### *Circumstances*

I always make sure that actors know the circumstances their characters are facing. By "circumstances," I mean the world of action that shapes the performance in a given moment. PTA provides the facts that anchor the scene in the real world. Circumstances take this one step further because they can be factual or imaginary. Since acting and directing are art forms and not science, imaginary circumstances are like the hidden wires and doors of a magic trick. The audience never has to see them, but they are intrigued by the result.

Always let the actor do it their way first. Watch and listen to the raw interpretation of the material, then work with what they have presented. The term for this is **giving an adjustment.** The best way to give an adjustment is to tweak the action or the circumstances or use any of the other directing tools in this chapter. Instead of "pick up the pace," I often say, "You've got moments to save a life." If an actor is overly emotional, I might encourage them to focus on their scene partner and "break through to their humanity. Hold your feeling back so THEY can feel something." When there are important player instructions, "Spell it out for the other character so they don't make a mistake. Make sure they get every detail, and study them as you speak to make certain it's registering." These are imaginative ways to speak to the actor to stimulate their inner work. If this seems complicated or out of reach to you as a director, just let it wash over you right now. This is not a set of rules that can't be broken. It's a way of talking that takes into account the training actors have. You will come to understand it in time.

My teacher Ned Manderino, author of *The Transpersonal Actor*, worked extensively with Lee Strasberg at The Actor's Studio. His technique employed deeply personal sensory work and actions, taken to a far-out spiritual level. I once asked him how I, as an actor, could respond to an adjustment from a director without going into an automatic cliché. His answer has stayed with me many years: "As long as you are responding to something internal, there will be a level of authenticity and the moment will be truthful."

Actors are trained to take risks, to be emotionally open, to perform, and to change what they are doing depending on the director's wishes or what they are getting from the other actor. They are depending on the director to hold the overview of the script and to help shape the dynamics of their performance through helping them to know the circumstances.

*Never give an actor a line reading*. Once you go down that road, you rob actors of their power. They are trained to bring the words to life in a way that is unique to them, which is what you are paying them for. Let them try things. Allow them to do their job of bringing it to life. Prepare and do all the homework. Come in with all your directorial ideas but hold them loosely. Very loosely. Then, let those ideas go. Don't try to hammer a performance out of an actor. You aren't merely using them as tools that say lines the way you tell them to.

There are so many pressures on a director that it's easy to take short cuts, to start giving line readings, to give only technical notes. If you, as a director, are falling back on "faster, funnier, more color" kind of direction, challenge yourself. Working with an actor is like having an important conversation. You might prepare for that conversation by thinking about what you want to say and the way you hope the other person will respond, but you can't memorize the conversation before it happens—all you can do is be prepared and then be in the moment. You can certainly draw on your preparation if it's useful, but in the moment, you might find yourself at a loss for words. Or something you never thought of comes up that's even better than what you had planned. It's OK to stop and think of a way to communicate creatively, respectfully, and in acting language.

Suggest an action or imaginary circumstance. Give your actor something to respond to. Remember that the facts of the scene are important as a jumping off point, but they don't need to restrict you. For the director or actors, previous moments can be either factual or an imagined secret whispered in an actor's ear. Just as a spine can be secret and delicious, a previous moment that is whispered in an actor's ear can be pure fiction. I once told an actor playing a super-cool but desperate bounty hunter, "Your spouse just told you there's no food for the kids. You have to collect the reward." If the scene needs speeding up, "There's a taxi with the meter running in the driveway." About another character: "They know how big your gambling debts are." "You had sex with them one drunken night and never discussed it." "She accused you of being a negligent mother." "You just found evidence they are a double agent." These can be made-up concepts that plant the seeds of a response in the actor using imaginative language.

This is your craft as a director.

### *As If*

An "as if" is a way of getting actors to inhabit the scene emotionally by using their imaginations rather than the direct circumstances of the scene. Violence, murder, espionage, zombie attacks? Most of these are not experiences the everyday actor has lived through.

The "as if" tool gives you a way out of the story-as-written into imaginative human experience. It's great to use if an actor is having trouble connecting with a scene. An "as if" makes the scene personal for actors, giving them an avenue to "be themselves" under particular circumstances. Here are some examples of "as if" directions:

- "As if you had just split your trousers."
- "As if you had just proposed and they said yes."
- "As if you came home and your entire family had been slaughtered in their beds."

These prompts are a better way to suggest possibilities to an actor than to bluntly ask for shock, concealed embarrassment or joy. This tool can be sensory as well. Here's one I often use to get someone to talk slightly louder but not shout: I'll say, it's "as if you were talking over a vacuum cleaner." For certain efforts—the small sounds required to bring life to the physicality of videogame characters—I'll use "as ifs" such as:

- "As if you were walking on sharp stones in bare feet."
- "As if someone had punched you in the gut."
- "As if your death scream was a warning to others."

The benefit here is that it not only engages the actor to talk louder but encourages them to communicate the information and thus changes the delivery in a very holistic manner.

### *Sensory Choices*

You are sitting in a café with a cup of tea. You dip a small soft cake—a madeleine—into the tea and take a bite. Suddenly you are transported, almost against your will, to your childhood. Previously blocked memories awaken so powerfully that you spend almost 4,000 pages telling your story. The taste of "Proust's madeleine" is the sensory trigger that starts one of the greatest 20th-century French novels, *A Remembrance of Things Past.*

Haven't you cracked a book, pulled out a photo, or opened a box and been immediately taken back to another time by the sight or smell? Or what about conjuring your "happy place" by creating or remembering the sense details of your favorite spot or activity? With our emphasis on giving the actor something to respond to, sensory choices are a fast, powerfully evocative tool. They are the secret tunnel in the Vatican that takes you right to the Sistine Chapel without having to wander through gallery after gallery of treasures.

If an actor doesn't feel comfortable with you probing into their private connections to the script, sensory choices are a safe suggestion that can be easily discarded if they don't work. I recently directed an actor in an interrogation scene where her action was "to gain the prisoner's trust so I can get the info out of them." In the first pass, the actor's choices left the prisoner staring straight ahead, unresponsive and defiant. I suggested she try a sensory choice of warm sunshine pouring out of her body toward the prisoner. On the second pass of the scene, the interrogation turned into a tender discussion between cautious friends and the prisoner couldn't help but give up some intel.

Visual sensory choices can be images such as a painting, a color, or a scene. An imaginary sound can evoke detailed character nuances. We used a lot of these in *Wolfenstein: The New Order*. For the scene set in a psychiatric asylum, one of the actors imagined a buzzing sound and voices that he kept swatting away like insects. In another scene, Several of the main characters swam through a cold sewer pipe and then, freezing and wet, waited outside the door of a hidden bunker. Just before the cameras started rolling, I led the actors in a short concentration exercise remembering the physical sensations of being cold. When we called *action*, they were right there with a full-on sense of place and environment.

Work with sensory choices carefully; too many, and your actor is so busy responding to inner sensory stimuli they are no longer in the moment playing the scene.

### *Obstacle*

Some of us need pressure to perform. When I have less time to get tasks done, I get more done in a shorter period of time. Athletes need to compete or they lose their edge. An obstacle is a great way to create a dynamic in a scene and to avoid the sin of overplaying. Obstacles can be factual or in the form of an "as if." An adjustment with an obstacle might be:

- Befriend him, but don't let him suspect you are a bounty hunter who will collect a big reward.
- Find the prisoner's cell, but don't alert the guards or set off an alarm.
- Make them understand the urgency of your situation but stay calm and collected so you can communicate.

When you give an actor an obstacle, script-based or imaginary, it increases the tension in the moment. If you put your thumb over a running hose, you get a high-powered spray that has force and tension. With an obstacle, the actor doesn't leap to the result of the scene but lives the process of it. By pushing answers back, obstacles make questions more interesting. Complications create interest.

*Personalization/Affective Memory*

Personalization is a way of asking, "What is this like for me?" While this is usually described as an acting exercise, a director can also use it to find interesting and fresh behaviors for characters in scenes. What is the essence of the internal experience, regardless of whether you have ever been in a similar situation? Finding "what it's like for me" brings out ideas that a director can use to describe their vision of a moment to the actor. Telling an actor, "When I was a kid, I was once humiliated by…" leads to a personal story that might trigger an actor's own personal connection. Connecting can be contagious.

Videogames contain many situations that are far beyond the experiences of normal humans. Most of the actors I encounter have not run through an exploding battlefield or ever murdered someone. How can personalization help an actor connect authentically when they've never had these experiences to draw on? But almost everyone has been to a club where the music is so loud that you must scream to be heard. And is there anyone who hasn't had a mosquito land on their arm and had the instinctive impulse to quickly and murderously end that insect's life?

The point here is that the actual specifics of the scene don't matter—only that the actor and director are able to extract the universality of human experience and apply it to the scene to bring it to life.

The affective memory exercise is one of the foundations of Method acting. Using the sensory cues of an actual memory, an actor can experience the emotions that occurred at key moments in their past in real time. Students in one of my classes did an affective memory on joy, honing in on the imagery, the sounds, and the smells of a particular experience. One described his last summer at home before leaving for college: "It's a warm summer day. I can smell the trees, the lawn. My father, my brother and I are painting our house. My father, so capable, so patient, is doing all the steps correctly. He is showing me how to do it. I can smell the paint and hear the music on the radio. I have this feeling of joy, of men working side by side to take care of the family…" His voice broke and he couldn't speak. Everyone listening was equally moved. Stanislavsky called this phenomenon "radiations," invisible waves of emotional energy that transfer to other actors and the viewer.

Directors can also delve into their past and re-experience feelings as a way of keying into what they are asking actors to access in emotional moments. When I connect with my own emotions internally and effortlessly generate waves of emotion (without indulging in expressing), my actors are more easily able to access their own emotions. I have my own name for this phenomenon: the *presence* of emotion.

### *Substitution*

One of the simplest personalizations is to make a substitution. An actor substitutes someone in their life for the person they are playing the scene with. They might pick a person they have strong feelings about, especially if the character they are playing has strong feelings about another character. The substitution might help them open up and create vulnerability or intimacy. It could also give them the ability to depersonalize their connection to another actor, as if they are a stranger. The acting community is small and tight, especially in games, and many actors may already have a history with each other. If they have to play an attraction to another character, they may need to make a substitution to generate the required erotic heat. If an actor is having trouble connecting with a scene partner, one of the first questions is always, "Have you made a substitution?"

In Robert Lewis' book, *Method or Madness*, he recounts asking actor Jacob Ben-Ami how he created a stunning moment in which his character, intending to commit suicide, draws a gun and aims it at his head. Lewis reports that the audience gasped in seeing the look on the actor's face. What personal moment was Ben-Ami drawing on at that moment? The most painful thing he could anticipate: stepping into an ice cold shower.

*Improvisation*

The most powerful directing tool I use is improvisation. For me, improvisation is a way of life. Even a well-rehearsed, carefully constructed scene must feel like an improvisation. I often remind actors after the first take, "This has never happened before, and this is the first time you are saying this." When takes feel stale, I ask the actors to improvise on the scene, to "free it up" with no restrictions or obligations. Once freed from the corset of expectation, new energies infuse the scene with life.

What does improvisation mean in an interactive piece, where often the narrative must tightly hew to specific parameters based on carefully coded development specs? In my many years of working on videogames, every kind of scenario has presented itself. Often, the creators have little-to-no experience in dramatic or comedic narrative, and they attempt to express their creative ideas along the lines of familiar tropes and borrowed ideas from television and film. "This is my John Carpenter moment, this is like in *Friends*, this is like when Luke gets imprisoned by Jabba the Hut…" I've worked with some of the most talented and creative people in the world, and it's frustrating when they try to shove their ideas into these formulaic boxes. (Well, sometimes they're being pushed to put them in boxes by the people who have decision-making power.) The fact is, unless you're John Carpenter or Steven Spielberg, you are not likely to successfully reproduce their work without having started from the same creative freedom they originally brought to it. Improvising—even in the most tightly scripted of player directions—opens a window into that creative freedom.

Fortunately, when shown other possibilities, most creatives and designers jump to fresh ideas. But there is frequently a holdout: the person who labored over the stock line or phrase and doesn't want to give it up. In such situations, it's usually best for actors and directors first to honor the wishes of these team members and attempt to reproduce what they've written or planned. If it doesn't work, it's usually clear to them right away. At least you've tried it.

Now, you have the freedom to improvise—and an improvisation on the material usually shows immediate promise. If you're reading this and are one of those people clinging to your ideas for dear life, I urge you to LET GO. Value your ideas but play with them, experiment with the situation, throw the pieces in the air, and take a risk. You'll only be better for it in the end, and your carefully crafted ideas may re-form with only slight adjustment. You can always go back to the old way, but I bet you won't want to.

Improvisation also adds an aura of risk. In a working scene, as in life, a character does not know exactly what the other characters will say or how they'll respond. Sometimes I hear an actor say, "I need my scene partner to give me such and such so I can respond in the right way." I shudder when I hear this, because it means the actor has locked in an expression or emotion which will certainly not feel fresh or spontaneous to the viewer. (They are also crossing a boundary, dictating how the other performer needs to act.) The game player, under most conditions, will be seeing and hearing this moment for the first time. However, in games, as in films, repeated viewing or playing means these emotional moments need to have even more spontaneous life beneath the carefully chosen words. I haven't heard of a game with entirely improvised scenes, but I certainly would love to direct one. In fact, I have a few times pitched the idea of improvising with actors under a set of circumstances, and only then designing the game around the characters. No one has taken me up on it … yet.

Improvisations can be entirely free-form, but the best I've experienced have a structure. Professional improvisers have very specific structures in place before they go out on stage. Like a good subtext, they're usually hidden enough that the audience marvels at the clever spontaneity of the performers. The most obvious is when the audience is prodded for "a place, a part of the body, a disgusting food," etc., as these become the structural elements for the improvisational sketch. Similar rules apply when utilizing improv as a dramatic or comedic tool in an interactive narrative. When the lines feel stiff, I invite an improvisation in the actors' own words. I would argue that in order for an improvisation to be effective, a structure is needed. In my work, that usually means a clear action. Once an actor has an action or a desired outcome, paired with another actor with a conflicting action, the foundations of a good improvisation are in place. A scene can be rewritten on the spot.

For in-game dialogue, which may encompass thousands and thousands of lines, an actor's improvisation can be a wonderful asset in keeping lines fresh. Many games have the same set of prompts for every in-game character. Letting an actor improvise on them can tailor this material to individual characters and help to bring the world of the game alive. Be aware, though, that improvisation doesn't automatically work for everyone.

I once had a very talented sound designer on a project insist that the auditioning actors improvise in-game battle chatter. I told the designer that some very good actors aren't comfortable improvising, especially if they don't play videogames. At the very least they need a structure. To give the auditioners a starting point, I collected a set of battle lines and encouraged the actors to try them out and then utilize them in an improvisation. For some actors, even changing a single word from the written text constitutes an improv. Anyone can improvise. Every time we talk to another person we are improvising. What makes it possible is knowing the topic of conversation and having a point of view. All the basics of a good scene.

You can use your own improvisations when preparing and doing research on a project. Outside the confines of the watchful eyes of producers, directors, animators, and minders of all kinds, you are free to explore the character and the dialogue in every direction. I have many times acted out scenes in my office, living room or garden. On my feet, or at a table using little dolls or even coins as characters, I argue with myself, playing both sides of a scene. These private explorations always yield insightful discoveries.

After you have given yourself the freedom to explore on multiple levels, it's imperative to go back to the choices and check that they serve the story, the level, the scene, and the beat. PTA is a big part of that evaluation. Once PTA has been established, you can use these other techniques to unlock the potential of a script and raise it above mere **illustration**.

I've seen actors do a marvelous improvisation on the lines and the scene, and then when switching back to the written dialogue, they immediately begin to speak their lines exactly how they did before the improv. All of us, even actors who have trained to avoid it, tend to revert back to the comfortable and conventional. We develop habits of body and voice that are hard to break. It's challenging but necessary to free ourselves from these patterns. Liberating the actor from the tyranny of illustrating the words allows the discoveries of improvisation to bring new reads to the same words.

Developers can also fall prey to **habituation**. A number of times I've experienced circumstances where an unqualified performer, usually a member of the development team, has stood in for a professional actor in recording placeholder dialogue. This substandard placeholder dialogue ends up in the game because the team has become so used to hearing it, they can't imagine any other interpretation.

### *Finding Truth in Emotional Moments*

Sometimes, a scene calls for a moment of emotional intensity, such as a breakdown, an argument, a tantrum, a celebration, or a deep expression of grief. The emotion is so strong that it seems to overwhelm the basic facts of PTA, raising the danger of overplaying. But if the actor is connected truthfully to the emotion in themselves, the scene will come together. While I was working on one sci-fi game, a lead actor had a monologue about the death of his wife from the effects of gamma radiation caused by his character's experiments. The script called for him to be sobbing over the corpse of his wife, but it didn't feel authentic for this actor to be sobbing. When the script calls for emotional responses, they should always be held lightly. If the scripted emotions cannot be delivered truthfully, something has to change. All the tools we've discussed in this chapter can help the actor and director see the same scene with the same words in a new light—one the actor can connect with.

In the sci-fi game, it was more authentic for the actor to have the character to cast himself as the true victim, filled with rage, shifting the blame for his wife's death onto the naysayers who wouldn't fund his research. If, as a director, I hadn't been flexible enough to see that, I would have spent considerable time trying to nudge my actor toward an inauthentic emotional reaction just because the script says so. Final choices must come out of the moment of rehearsal and performance, when the scene is being acted out. In my view, even writers serve the material well by holding it loosely and being open to what happens on the set.

When an extreme emotional moment is called for at an exact spot in the script, actors have a tendency to spend the entire scene working up to that moment, taking the spontaneity out of everything else they do. Why sacrifice every moment of the scene for one gushing release? If they know that authenticity is the most important ingredient of their emotional response, they are likely to be much freer in playing every moment of the scene up until that point.

Directors need to be particularly sensitive to actors performing emotional moments. A supportive presence is absolutely required. Make sure the actor has everything they need and that all the PTA and circumstances of the script are very clear. Rehearse emotional scenes casually, without expending a lot of emotion on them, and make sure that all technical considerations are as locked down as possible. You don't want a great emotional take ruined by an avoidable technical or blocking or prop mistake. Like a rare orchid, the opportunity to create an authentic emotional moment is uncommon, precious, and easy to kill. Handle it with care.

As a director, allow yourself to experience the emotions of the actors simultaneously in your own body. Sometimes the entire crew is crying during very emotional scenes. This can be a wonderful thing if everyone is able to do their jobs. But actors are usually very tuned in to how the director feels, and when you are feeling it, they are feeling it. And if the emotions start to run dry or feel stale or pushed, ease off. Look for other nuances in less showy takes.

Authenticity and truth are the rule of the day, particularly for emotional moments.

**BOX 5.1: Case Study: Jimmy Carver in Wolfenstein II**

During production of *Wolfenstein II: The New Colossus*, creative director Jens Matthies really wanted me to get in the suit and portray a character. Having been an actor and studied acting for many years, I was excited by the prospect but daunted at appearing next to the high level of talent I was working with in my acting ensemble. I thought of perhaps a small walk-on, but Jens insisted on having me play the character of Jimmy Carver, a 1960s talk show host in the vein of Johnny Carson, on whose show the player has the final boss battle and must kill the villain, the evil Nazi Frau Engel.

Fortunately, I had a wonderful scene partner in Nina Franoszek who played Frau Engel. During the scene, the talk show host both humanizes and glorifies Frau Engel, but between takes on the fictional show, it is revealed his life is at stake in selling Frau Engel to the public as a beloved leader. During my prep sessions, I asked myself, "Does Jimmy Carver believe what he's saying about Frau Engel?" I decided to play him as if he were one of the Americans who believed a Nazi takeover of the US was a good thing indeed. My next question was, "What is this situation like for me, even if imagined?"

I tried a particular kind of improvisation—also a classic "as if"—and imagined an interview with Barbra Streisand, who has a reputation as a notoriously fussy diva. As an admirer of Ms. Streisand's singing, I would find it natural to praise her, and the prospect of offending her would be daunting. I kept working with my own improvisation of such a scene, in my own words, and then, without changing the emotional tone I'd developed in my improv, I returned to the words in the script. Now the script was secretly enriched by my imaginary interview with Barbra. Once I had that down, Nina and I were able to make the interview seem like a fun chat between old friends. But when the scene shifted to the host and celebrity interacting during a commercial break, Nina's character had to reestablish her power with life-threatening criticisms. The scene was massively fun to shoot, and our prep work served us well. I saw one player's comment, "That scene made me nervous!"

The ability to assess each actors' gifts and talents and put them to use in service of the project is the core of the director's work. All of these tools have one thing in common: they respect the actors' process as collaborators. Using actor language marks a director as a supporter and ally of the actor. Giving adjustments in actor language is a creative discipline that shows you are an artist who has honed their craft.

## References

Johnstone, Keith. *Impro: Improvisation and the Theatre*. Routledge, 1987.
Lewis, Robert. *Method—or Madness?* Samuel French, Inc., 1958.
Manderino, Ned. *The Transpersonal Actor: Reinterpreting Stanislavski*. Manderino Books, 1976.
Manderino, Ned. *All About Method Acting*. Manderino Books, 1985.
Manderino, Ned. *Actor as Artist*. Manderino Books, 1991.
Spolin, Viola. *Improvisation for the Theater: A Handbook of Teaching and Directing Technique*. Northwestern University Press, 1963.
*Wolfenstein II: The New Colossus.* Machine Games/Bethesda Softworks, 2017.

# 6
# The Director's Most Important Job

**In This Chapter**

- The way of the director
- A director's vision
- Radical specificity
- Self, society, and culture
- All experience is local
- Truth, lies, good, and evil

You've been reading this book because you are, or you want to be, a director. Maybe as a kid you were putting on shows or making movies. Or you've been an actor, or an animator, or a writer, and you've been involved in a production and you think, "I could do that." We've discussed a lot of techniques for working with actors. But the director's path is a unique one. How far are you willing to go? What is it that excites you about directing and how can you nourish and deepen it?

You find the director within yourself the way a sculptor finds an image in the marble. It's about knowing the relationship between material and world and studying both with fine attunement and a sharp chisel. There is no one thing a director looks like. It took me a long time, decades even, to become the director I am today. Because of what I perceived was a lack in my training—a solid grounding in psychologically realistic acting—I was driven by a passion to crack the stone of acting and directing. I had many great teachers along the way, and each step on the process was a shearing force that eventually broke open the diamond. No one can say when that process happens for an individual artist. Some are fortunate to come on it very young. Some


DOI: 10.1201/9781003558910-7

have a gradual dawning based on moments in a scene that glow with life. Some crack it all at once in an astonishing revelation.

What is the most important job of the director? You may think it's your script analyses, your actions, your shot lists, your blocking ideas, your design concepts, and your casting sensibility. Certainly, all those things are important, no question. But having directed theater, dance, voiceover, film, and performance, I found out the *real* job of the director in one of those experiences that pulled everything together for me.

### The Way of the Director

As I mentioned before, after a few years as an "inside" employee in the videogame industry, I began to investigate what our company called "professional development." There was, it turned out, money available for classes that directly contributed to employees doing their jobs better. Having been an actor, dancer, and choreographer, I know the discipline of "going to class." Dancers take a class of some sort on almost daily basis in order to keep their technique sharp. Actors dive into acting classes to refresh their technique, get feedback, drop any clichés or habits they may have picked up, and work on material that may be above and beyond the fare they get to play commercially.

Since the company was offering classes, I began to wonder, where do *directors* take class? How often do directors get to work? Some directors work all the time, but many may go months or years developing projects without actually getting in front of actors. How do directors keep from getting stale? The reality is that it's hard for directors to find a place. This was when I searched the internet and, in a moment of serendipity, found Judith Weston. I was immediately taken by the fact that Judith required her directing students to take her basic acting class, study scene analysis, and eventually take her Actors and Directors Lab. That Lab was where I came to the most profound understanding of myself as a director.

Each week, directors would either be assigned a scene or bring in a scene of their own choosing. They would be assigned actors, some of whom were directors as well, such as myself. The idea was that the director and the actors made the scene work, no matter who was cast and whether they were right for the role or not. A scene with Hamlet and the ghost might become about a daughter with a father who had turned into a zombie. I enjoyed the acting part as much as the directing, since my roots were in acting.

There was a fellow who hung around the class, usually standing in the back. He had an accent I couldn't define. He spoke very little, and usually, it was just friendly small talk. But his presence and his eyes had a weight and a nameless pain that gave him depth. I didn't even know if he was actually a student, until one week it was announced that Joseph was doing a scene and he needed actors. I gamely signed up, along with a 40ish actress, without knowing what was in store because that was the vibe of the class.

The scene he had chosen turned out to be something out of an after-school melodrama. A teenager who has cut her wrists is visited in the hospital by an angel who turns out to be her deceased father. I immediately seized on an intuitive idea for the character. I would do it in an Irish accent, and wear a heavy overcoat, like the angels in the Wim Wenders film *Wings of Desire*. See, I already had the coat and I could do an Irish accent of sorts, just like my Irish relatives who had come over in the 1960s with their thick tweed jackets and shoes and their cigarettes at funerals. "Ah, Tommy, such a shame about your poor mother. Lord have mercy on her soul…"

Each group had one rehearsal allotted before they showed the work in class, as if the showing were the second rehearsal. The actress and I showed up with Joseph and began to rehearse the scene. Joseph's directing skills were not strong. He seemed hesitant to give us any adjustments. We were floundering with the material. The actress broke down first. She stopped in the middle of the scene and faced us both. "What are we doing here? What is this? Me, playing a teenager? And him," pointing at me, "with the accent?" Like a sea anemone that had just had a stick thrust into it, I felt myself reflexively closing down. What had I been thinking with this accent? And this stupid coat? We all took a break and went to our respective corners to lick our wounds. We ran through the scene again in a dutiful, lifeless way, and the rehearsal was over.

The protocol for the presentation in class with Judith was that you would present the scene, and then the actors and the director would sit on stage with Judith, and she would ask the actors, "What was it like to work with this director?" This was sometimes the most painfully honest feedback a director would ever get, and I learned so much from it. When she asked us about working with Joseph, there was an awkward silence. I plunged in and outlined the events as I saw them. Judith turned to Joseph. "Why did you pick this scene?"

Joseph paused, took a deep breath, and began to speak. "Years ago, when I left my country because of the war, I was escorted over the mountains by a drug mule. They said he was my uncle, but he wasn't. At one point, we were stopped and held captive by a rival cartel. They wanted the names of relatives they could pressure to get money for us. If they didn't pay up, we would be killed. Even if they did, we would probably have been killed anyway. In the middle of the night, me and some of the others got away and hid in the jungle. We had to go a long way, on foot, and at one point I didn't think I could go on. I began to pray. I prayed to my older brother, my big brother, who had already died trying to make this same crossing. I heard his voice saying, 'Hold on. Hold on Joseph ... you can make it.' He was an angel, guiding me. Miraculously, some people from a church found us, gave us food, and got us out of there. And here I am today."

"Did you tell your actors this?" Judith asked gently.

Joseph looked down.

"Why not?"

Then Judith spoke to all of us: "You have to share what this material means to you. How can you expect your actors to open up when you have not? You open up and you make a space where it's safe for everyone to open up, to draw on their experiences and their imagination. *The director sets the tone for the entire production.*"

Judith looked at Joseph. "Let's take it again," she said.

We did the scene. This time, that small, after-school-special had the weight and depth of Shakespeare. It was a lightning bolt for me. I realized how often I had not even explored or articulated my own connection to the script, leaving the actors in the dark as to what was fueling my adjustments to their work.

Since that unforgettable experience in Judith's class, I always identify the themes in the piece and then do the "as ifs" to personalize it. I look deeply and honestly to see what experiences I have that open me up to unforgettable choices, and I share my ideas with my actors. As the late director Jean Marc Valle said about his work, "You've got to create a space where they're going to feel respected and comfortable ... in order to capture something that feels real and authentic." Too many directors have no experience with the craft of directing and focus all their attention on getting shots, shots and shots and shots, leaving the actors to fill in the acting piece on their own.

*Director's Vision*

One key way a director sets the tone for a production is to communicate their vision. *A vision is not only visual.* It involves mood, sound, and rhythm. But where does something as diffuse as vision come from, and at what point in the process does the director commit to it? It's important here to understand that a vision is organic and flexible. It begins to form even on the director's first reading of the script, when the material is new and its force and implications are most freshly felt.

Once a vision begins to form, some directors create an actual vision board covered with images, photos, or paintings, serving as both inspiration and a way of communicating their ideas. I myself have collected images and even used the composition of classical paintings as inspiration for blocking. Research is another of my key tools; the internet is the director's friend. Almost every psychological archetype and relationship has an illuminating article about it somewhere online.

For example, while researching a game set in 1930s Europe, I found a book written by a woman who had her American parents' travel diary from Germany in 1937. She researched what current events were transpiring at the time her folks wrote things like, "missed train…lost baggage" and connected the dots into a fascinating narrative about conditions in pre-war Germany. This is how a director builds a vision. I've built my vision for productions around audio, a movement style, and even classical theater.

How do you find your own way to set the tone for your production? Is it the way you begin the table read, giving everyone permission to fail? Is it a call with each cast member to discuss the role in advance? Is it with a warmup? Is it a circle with just the actors in which each shares their connection to the story? If I don't get the time do one or all of these, it's often harder to crack the scenes and build a feeling of a rich ensemble. Too much energy is wasted while the actors circle around, looking for an anchor of safety.

But the performance director of a game does not have the freedom to install their vision wholesale; rather, the vision must eventually be shaped to match the dynamics of the production team's vision. Games are almost never the place for a grand auteur. In some cases, the videogame performance director's domain doesn't include the actual visuals or sound score for a scene. As a performance director, you can't always paint and score the world of the game, but if you communicate your vision well, you'll influence the team members who can.

The opening scene for *Battlefield 4* is a case in point. A vision for the scene came to me out of my director's prep. Analyzing the PTA gave me an idea. The player is in a sinking car with two squad mates and their commanding officer. The scene on paper was written with a lot of "shouty" panic and hysteria, but I knew that wouldn't work.

"In a sinking car," I told the actors, "The most precious resource is air, so whatever you do, make sure you are conserving it. No unnecessary shouting that might use it up."

After we shot the scene with that adjustment, everyone agreed the scene had a very good tension and closeness. However, when the team took the raw material from the scene back to the studio, the feedback was, "That's it?" The scene didn't yet have any music or dynamics of the artwork, and it came off flat.

But the team defended our decision. Set to Bonnie Tyler's song *Total Eclipse of the Heart*, inside a small car with the sound and visuals of air bubbling out of the slowly fracturing windows, the final result was gripping and filled with dread. It was anything but flat.

A vision can be sound, a vision can be graphics, a vision can be a way of working. The important thing for a director is to have a vision that connects you, the artist, to the universality of human experience. Your job, your *craft*, is to share that vision with the development team and the actors in an open and collaborative environment.

### *Translating Your Vision*

How do we avoid the clichés of behavior and find the interesting, original and nuanced expressions of life that mark memorable performances? Every actor, director, and animator who wishes to do so must become an observer and student of human behavior. The hardest thing about this process is self-examination. What do we really feel and experience? What rumbles beneath the veneer of everyday activity and communication? I say that all experience is local, meaning that experience can be understood as an everyday occurrence of some kind.

But what lies underneath those everyday experiences?

*Radical Specificity*

In acting and directing, it's important to know the true meaning of **specificity**. When I say to an actor, "Make it specific," I'm asking them to find a connection that is full of nuance, rather than a generalized expression. It's always easy, tempting, and dangerous to default to a generic emotion.

For example, imagine you want to express "sad" in a watercolor painting. Well, you could coat the entire background of the painting with, say, a deep blue wash. But later, wouldn't we want to paint something over it, or look for nuances in the color field with more or less paint, or the texture of the brush? Wouldn't you want to imagine or summon an actual nuanced moment or experienced mood to put on paper, whether it's abstract or figurative? The key is in the complication.

It's the same for emotional moments in performance. A **generalized expression** of "sad" might involve a downturned mouth, limp, collapsed expression in the body, and low voice. That's what I call "illustrating" sadness. But, instead of a generalized expression, how can we make sadness specific? A good place to start is at our own behavior. What behavior does a specific sadness call forth? When a loved one passes or a career opportunity is lost, aren't there more nuanced expressions than a frown in our behavior? For example, in my own life, some years ago, my brother was suffering from an incurable illness. I went with him and my mother to the doctor's appointment, where we were told, "There's nothing more we can do. Go home and be comfortable."

There's a shock and finality to hearing those words. What were our behaviors? My brother just sat still. My mother went into overdrive. "Ice cream. We have to have ice cream!" I became the enabler, mapping our route to the ice cream parlor. How does that compare to a turned down mouth? It's far superior, even adding a comic element. What other behaviors do humans exhibit when faced with sadness and loss? The numbness that comes with having to soldier on, alive, without the deceased? The shock that comes with an unexpected turn? The fondness and closeness to the deceased? Or even the freedom that comes with a release from a particular obligation or relationship? All of these create *specific* moments relating to an event, instead of the kind of clichéd, generic, *illustrated* response upon which so much entertainment rests, especially in videogames.

**BOX 6.1: Generalized Reactions**

What is to be done when a *producer* asks for generalized, stock reactions from talent? Of course, every situation is different. Personally, I've used specificity to spark a more nuanced discussion with a producer who makes that type of request. When I've had these kinds of discussions in the past, it's because the producer is afraid to take a risk and be criticized by the rest of the team. Usually, I suggest we try the more nuanced idea as an alternative so we have both versions and everyone is happy. And more often than not, the more nuanced version ends up in the game.

### Self, Society, and Culture

As part of the artist's study of humanity and human nature, it's a useful exercise to consider some clear-eyed questions about yourself. The late casting director Sam Christensen developed a process, still in use at his studio today, sending teams of actors out into the public together to survey people on the street as to how an actor is perceived. The actor would stand at a distance and be observed by the public, who would be questioned by the team about what they perceived as the character, age, profession, and marital status of the actor, with whom they had no contact. At our stage in life, how are we perceived by people? What is our goal in life, and how are we going about achieving it? What are our most important preoccupations? Also, historically, what have been the biggest influences that have shaped our view of the world? Are our own values shared by everyone?

I once attended a presentation about trends where several generations of Americans were divided into subgroups based on the biggest influences on their lives. Folks growing up or just coming of age during the Great Depression of the 1930s were heavily influenced by the need for security. Those alive during World War II had a tremendous need for stability and a "traditional home." Kids brought up in 1950s America and Europe wanted to break out of that cloying stability, and the social revolution of the 1960s was born. Generation X, born in the 1970s, saw their parents' careers derailed by layoffs and the end of employer/employee loyalty. Different cultures and nations have different influences, but most humans do respond in the same way to the factors that influence them. Meanwhile, each generation has its own set of repressed ideas and emotions. Depending on the social norms of their world, the shadow will be all that was unexpressed.

Investigate the commonalities and differences in cultures by talking to people, reading, and absorbing what it's like to stand in another's shoes. If we had on different shoes, how would we respond? A man may mock the way a woman runs in high heels, but if he slipped them on no doubt he would run in a similar fashion.

### *All Experience Is Local*

All experience is **local** and can be understood as an everyday occurrence of some kind. While characters may have a grand idea or desire for their life at this time—their *spine*—the pursuit of it is like someone crossing a river on their way to save the world. They still have to cross the river! That means making their way over water and stones and sand, perhaps being chased in the process.

Whether a character is on a spaceship, in a tank, or at a gas station, they still must attend to local, immediate human activities, such as those rocks on the way across the river. In acting terms, the life of the character is told in these small, local, *specific* moments.

When fleshing out a character, I always make a short list of the facts I know about the character from the script and from any materials the team has given me. I call those the known facts. Then I make a list of all the questions I have about the local aspects of the character's life:

- Where do they live?
- Who do they listen to?
- Who cares about them?
- Where are their parents?
- How do they make a living?
- What kinds of stumbling blocks might they have encountered?

And then there are the really big questions:

- What do they desire in this life?
- What is the likely outcome of their life unless they make different choices?

- What is the likely outcome of their life if they do make different choices?
- Will they partner up and marry, have children?
- Where are they in their life's journey, and what will they do when they are old?
- Will they die soon, and do they have a premonition that they might not be around long?

The reality is that every human has similar characteristics in their existence. They are born and will die. They create relationships, they engage in tasks, they have unavoidable needs, immediate wants, and grand desires. The question, "What would anyone, in this situation, want to do?" is a powerful insight into the "local" quality of the character, which must always be kept in sight.

When an actor's moment feels generalized, overly broad, or cliché, an insightful director suggests an adjustment that gives the actor something specific to do. Something local. It grounds the moment and brings it alive in a simple way. Certain action verbs are more general than specific. As a young actor, I used to break down a script into what I thought were action verbs. "To walk across the room. To open the door. To get a drink of water. To answer her question." These "actions" are more like boring, superficial lists of the activities than performable action verbs. Even a verb like, "to convince" is a generalized action verb because it isn't specific. How would a character look when convinced? What does the character need to do or say to specifically change another character's mind? To gain their trust? To make them laugh? To put the fear of God in them?

There is no juice in pedestrian action verbs that merely describe the blocking or restate what the script says. If a verb is too broad it doesn't give the actor anything concrete or stimulating to play. A good director uses their imagination to turn the language into something juicy, fun, or daring, and then breaks that down into local behavior.

*In Star Wars Jedi: Survivor,* there's a scene where three characters pay their respects to the dead body of a fallen comrade. The actors, who had all worked together for years, were filled with genuine emotion. One of the actors felt lost, so I suggested an *as if*: "As if you were confronting a gigantic family problem that had absolutely no good solution." Grounded by this suggestion, the actor could substitute a real or imagined personal dilemma to make a connection and find authentic behavior from their own personal experience.

Our honest responses to life are so rich and unpredictable and—when examined and studied—they provide endless material. This is why I don't think artificial intelligence can ever match the complexity and experience carved into every single living, breathing, human being, and replace the human actor.

*Truth, Lies, Good, and Evil*

One tool that is a lot of fun to play with are the ideas of truth and lies. How much of what we tell people is the bare-bones, unvarnished truth? Whenever I'm breaking down a script, I like to play with these concepts and challenge every truth about a character to see where they might be lying. In one recent script I worked on, a mother on the run was working to convince another character that she was trustworthy. To prove her credentials as a refugee, she had to deliver a moving monologue about how her husband was unfairly convicted of a crime and put to death. I asked the actor playing the mother, "Do you think she's telling the truth about her husband? What if he was guilty after all?" This adjustment gave the actor more fuel for the emotional content of the monologue. She had to redeem him with her story. Later, in a second iteration of this game where the mother was no longer alive, it turned out the husband had survived and become a serial-killing monster.

Directors also need to challenge culturally assumed ideas of good and evil. Once, before the beginning of a project, I asked a famous actor if he had any questions about the script.

"Yeah," he said, "just one."

"OK, what is it?"

"Am I a good guy or a bad guy?"

What makes a character a good guy or a bad guy? Whether or not we genuinely believe a character is good or evil, every director and the actor playing the character must go beyond these conventional distinctions. On a local level, what makes the characters behave the way they do? What is driving their choices that makes them appear either good or evil to the general public? What is true about them and what are lies? It's a powerful actor who can dig into a villain and uncover the pain that makes the character believe that their "evil" choices are the best from the worldview they hold. Never make a judgment about a villain—you will only end up with a stock, cliché character.

Recently, I directed a short piece about a woman who abandons her husband and children. My first reaction was that she must be mad. How could anyone do that? My research led me to write about the nuances of women who leave their families. Conventionally, men get away with it, but women are called monsters. There's a clear double standard here that I only woke up to by researching the topic. I love these eye-opening moments, for they remind me to never judge a character.

In Jungian psychology, there is a concept called, **the shadow.** The shadow is all that is unexpressed within us, all that lies behind the mask we present to the world. As creative people, we have a duty and obligation to explore what's on the other side of the conventional tropes and stereotypes of heroes and villains. Actress Liv Ullman, who starred in many of Swedish director Ingmar Bergman's films, famously described how important it was to always create the other side of the character, the character behind the face. To see the suffering of a character, of humans, and not turn away. "Performances help you know what it is to be a human being," she said in an interview. "That's holiness."

One of the favorite tools I learned from Judith Weston is to do it "wrong." Pick an action or objective or want that is so ridiculously anti-correct to the intention of the scene. This is ultimately freeing and fun. Often the opposite of what is "supposed" to be played can lead to unusual "Why not?" insights. Why not let there be an erotic undertone when a character challenges another to a fight? Why not play a break-up scene with cool rationality, as if every statement were a proven fact? Why not let a character chuckle as they plead for their life? I often use these ideas when I'm brainstorming the spine of the character because they often lead me right to what the character's spine rightfully should be—juicy and filled with nuance. That's the power of exploring the shadow side of a character.

One could argue that videogames owe their power to allowing players to live out fantasy lives and perform acts that satisfy primal longings that still linger in the human psyche. But it's more than that: As the art of videogames develops, we'll find increasingly that it's not enough to offer players an opportunity to move into the life of a monster. What will matter are the nuances that make that character more than a monster, or less than one, or maybe not a monster at all. The same goes for the good guys.

### Game Time

Every human being is a mass of contradictions, hidden agendas, secret desires, vain hopes, glorious capabilities, weird attractions, heartfelt sympathies, good-natured willingness, and stubborn delusions. Embrace all of this in yourself and others. Don't fear the actors or the developers. Let the work be a group exploration of a story and people in time and space. Embrace the inconsistencies, the flaws, the light and shadows, and you will find a rich life in practicing the art of directing. Videogames offer directors a tremendous opportunity to get an enormous amount of face time with actors, both in the pcap volume and the voiceover booth. As a director, you are working as coach, mentor, psychologist, parent, guru, and friend. It is a life-long art that grows richer over time. Every session is an opportunity to practice and learn the subtle art of telling a story through the bodies and voices of humans.

## References

*Battlefield 4.* Developed by DICE, Electronic Arts, 2013.

Gray, Tim. "Liv Ullman Life Lessons." *Never Turn Away, Never Kill Somebody's Dream*, *Variety*, 1 Mar. 2021.

*Star Wars Jedi: Survivor.* Developed by Respawn Entertainment, Electronic Arts, 2023.

Tyler, Bonnie. "Total Eclipse of the Heart." *Faster Than the Speed of Night*, Columbia Records, 1983.

Vallee, Jean-Marc. "Working With Strong Female Leads." *Sharp Objects*, HBO, 19 July 2018.

Weston, Judith. *The Film Director's Intuition: Script Analysis and Rehearsal.* Michael Wiese Productions, 2003.

Weston, Judith. *Directing Actors: Creating Memorable Performances for Film and Television*. Michael Wiese Productions, 2021.

*Wings of Desire.* Directed by Wim Wenders, performances by Bruno Ganz, Solveig Dommartin, and Otto Sander, Metro-Goldwyn-Mayer, 1987.

Zweig, Connie, and Jeremiah Abrams, editors. *Meeting the Shadow: The Hidden Power of the Dark Side of Human Nature*. Jeremy P. Tarcher/Penguin Group, 1991.

# 7
# Casting the Videogame

**In This Chapter**

- How casting works
- What are breakdowns and character descriptions
- Working with a casting director
- Reviewing self-tapes and pre-screenings
- Holding live auditions and callbacks
- How to make selections

It's a dreary day in London, where I've come to cast male actors between 25 and 40 years old to play American soldiers. American soldiers in London? The developer is European and wants to do the performance capture locally. No problem, London is loaded with accomplished actors; it should be the place to be. But I'm not feeling confident. This is February 2010, and the pool of great British talents with fabulous American accents willing to enter the still-strange world of videogames is looking mighty shallow.

This is day two of four. My stomach is growling because it's almost lunchtime, and I have one more actor to see before I get food. I'm starting to panic because I've seen precious few possibilities so far. A sprinkling of Americans and a lot of Brits and Australians, whose weak Yankee accents tend to fall to New Yawk or Texas, y'all. One guy slides back and forth between them, throwing in a dash of Aussie for spice.

My final actor comes in, and he's centered and prepared. He's learned the lines for the scene. His American accent is flawless. He's taking direction from me and running with it. My excitement is growing. I know this guy is going to be hired for a role. The audition ends.

"Thank you very much," I say.

DOI: 10.1201/9781003558910-8

While the actor gathers up his things, I put my head down and massage my temples. "This guy is perfect," I'm thinking. "I need six of him. Where am I going to find them?"

The actor stops at the door and turns around to say something to me. As I look up, I catch his face and—I'll never forget this moment—I see myself through his eyes. They are the eyes of every actor who has ever auditioned. He's reading me, and he's reading me wrong. To his eyes, my body language says, "I'm so disappointed in what you just did." His happy face falls and his shoulders slump forward. Crestfallen. He will have a terrible afternoon feeling like a failure, feeling less than. He will shrug it off, bury it with all the other lost opportunities, and move on. A day, a week, or a month later, he will get a call offering him a job. He'll find it hard to believe because he was sure I hated him.

This is the life of an actor.

### Auditioning Actors

Actors at an audition have the sensitivity of finely tuned racehorses, their emotions bubbling just below the surface, strange words floating around in their brain, and their senses on high alert for cues from the director or producers. They've quickly examined the material they've received, come up with a few ideas, and practiced the scenes in front of a mirror in their bedroom. If they are lucky, they may get to do this several times a week, but each audition takes time and energy to prepare. They've picked out an outfit that fits the character but that maybe they can also wear to their day job or next audition without having to change on the street. They may have just dropped off their children at daycare or are running up a tab with a babysitter.

At a live audition, they've seen other versions of themselves in the waiting room, where they might hear the audition of the person before them leaking through the walls. When it's their turn, they have precious few minutes to greet and connect with the producing team, ask a few questions, show their best work, and make an unforgettable impression. As their characters, they may cry or rage or fight. Then it's time to get on with their day as if nothing had happened. They don't dare to get their hopes up because if they do, the loss of that hope can be soul-crushing.

I wish developers would understand that when they are casting, they're not shopping for goods. The amount of time an actor spends on an audition, preparing, memorizing the lines, getting ready, and showing up, accords the actor the right to respect. Even if the actor is not fit for the role, they may be right for something else at another time. I once watched an executive producer flip through headshots of women in the cruelest way: "Oh no, no, ugh ugly, oh my god no, maybe, yes she's hot…" The people he's dismissing have sacrificed a lot to bring the level of talent and training a developer is looking for in a performer.

In the popular imagination, actors are spoiled narcissists. Is this true? Well, pop-culture also pictures videogamers as overgrown couch potatoes living in their parents' basements. Is *that* true? If you're going to direct a videogame, you'll need to leave the clichés behind. Actors are artists and creators, much like the people who make games for a living. Some are the greatest on the planet, some are unhappy angry people, and most are somewhere in-between.

### What Are You Looking For?

When it comes to casting performers for a videogame, it's important to know what to look for: truthful acting, a strong and clear voice, a fluid and expressive face and body for performance capture, and the ability to respond and take direction. Increasingly, the actors' look and likeness are being scanned and used for the character design, adding another level of complexity to finding the right ingredients for the character. And on top of these foundational ingredients, flexibility and imagination are absolute requirements for actors who work on games.

Keep in mind the unique challenges videogame actors will have to face. For performance capture—at least at this moment in time—the actor will be covered by equipment from head to toe. They will be standing on a framework set with little to no visuals, no costumes, in a room with poor acoustical resonance, giving no audio feedback from their voice. They may be asked to deliver a few lines, and then "idle" for some seconds, and speak another set of lines with gestures, idle again, and repeat. Their previous moment might be something that has occurred, but then again, it might happen later, depending on the actions of the player. Bound by these constraints, the actors must bring their characters to life (Figure 7.1).

**Figure 7.1** Performance capture actors and crew shooting a sequence for *Indiana Jones and the Great Circle*. L to R: Alessandra Mastronardi, Troy Baker, Grace Voranath, "Pu" Vithaya Pansringarm, dolly grip Tony Perija, and director of photography Kyle Klutz. (Photo by Sigtor Kildal. Courtesy of Machinegames, ZeniMax, and Lucasfilm.)

Voice actors have other demands. They may not get any information about the project before their arrival at the studio. (Though I strongly suggest sending the scripts ahead of time, even for voice actors!) They may be asked to play multiple characters with completely different voices. And they most likely will be playing scenes without another actor to respond to. Each actor may also have to do a set of "efforts"—sounds that help bring the animated character to life. Lead characters do everything—the sounds of running, jumping, landing, choking, squeezing through narrow passageways, vomiting, dying over and over. In most zombie games, every actor must do a full set of zombie growls, squeals and screams. Actors may experience extreme vocal stress providing these sounds, and must know how to take care of their instrument so they don't change sound or lose their voice midway through the recording session.

A live casting session is the place for both actors and directors to see what they are getting into, and how it will be to work with each other. While there is currently a trend to rely exclusively on actors' self-tapes in casting, I feel that it's extremely important for the director to have an actual live interaction with them, whether it's remote or in person. Certain high-profile actors don't want to audition at all, but I let them know (as diplomatically as possible) that a test session is as important for them as well as for the producers, so the actors can see what the process is like before they commit to it.

At a recent callback, I asked the former star of a TV show, who just stood with his arms hanging at his side reciting his lines, to put some expression into those arms. He snapped back, "You're not going to ask me to overact, are you?" I explained that performance capture has more room for physical expression than what normally works on camera. A lot like theater acting, in fact. He countered that he prefers stillness in a performance on stage. I explained that in motion capture, some small movement is always required—even if just a slightly physicalized rise and fall of the breath—or the figure appears lifeless. "You know," I counseled him, "like an electric vehicle when it's waiting at a light. When it's not moving, it feels like it's died." By then, of course, we might as well have called it. An actor like that would never survive in a pcap volume because he was too rigid about his acting technique.

Casting is a two-way street. Not only are you offering a job, you are marketing the job to the acting community and their agents and managers. Remember that this medium is often new to them, and communicate thoughtfully through your materials. If you have hired a casting director, they can only work with what you give them. Be as specific as you can about what you're looking for. Learn what a **breakdown** is, what **sides** are, and what information the actor needs to know. Your materials are saying, "We are serious about this project, we are prepared to provide you with the direction and information for you to do your best work. We see you as a collaborator with our team."

### The Casting Process

How do we go about finding the right actor? What should you look for? What should you do in an audition and what is the best way to evaluate the auditions? Remember: *The right actor is one who easily and naturally brings the qualities you are looking for to the role.* Of course, first you will have to define those qualities, and that's where your breakdown or casting brief comes in.

### *The Breakdown*

In this phase, we literally break the script down into characters and all the information about those characters. For performance capture casting (usually considered "on-camera"), In the US there's a company called Breakdown Express that has for years been the industry standard for posting casting notices to agents and managers. (For voiceover casting, there's a smaller pool of agents and managers, so the breakdown usually goes directly to them.) Consider your breakdown the introduction to the project for the gatekeepers, the agents, and managers who will decide whether to submit their clients for these roles. For smaller projects where actors themselves may submit, the more specific the breakdown, the more likely the actor will submit for the appropriate role. Even when you are specific, some agents and actors will misread the breakdown. It's disconcerting when you post a call for a "30-year-old Black female," and a 55-year-old white guy is submitted for the role.

This may sound very basic, but remember that the easier you make it for someone to enter into your world, the better the relationship will be.

### *Creating the Breakdown or Casting Brief*

My casting director and I create breakdowns for our clients, but it's good for developers to know about the process too. Here's the anatomy of a breakdown:

- Short description of the project as a whole
  *e.g. Action/adventure videogame set in the future on a distant planet.*
- Union status
  e.g. **SAG/AFTRA, ACTRA, Equity, Non-Union**
- Publisher, Casting team, and Director
  *e.g. Electronic Arts, Emily Schweber, Tom Keegan*

- Deadlines for submissions of actor materials and where and what kind
  *e.g. Headshots and reels must be received at Emily Schweber casting by January 29th*
- Time and location of shooting
  *e.g. London, UK Spring of 2019 and with shoots extending into 2021*
- Pay rate
  *e.g. SAG/AFTRA Scale +10% or £250/hr. Overscale available for name talent*
- Contact info for questions
- Character name, gender, age range
  *e.g. Eloise, F, 35–45*
- Short but great description of the part
  *e.g. Interstellar bounty hunter seeking a big payday. Adopts various disguises so she can flaunt local laws and willing to bring in a prize "dead or alive."*
- Any physical, race or language requirements
  *e.g. Black, South Asian or mixed race. Athletic and knows how to handle a weapon.*

**BOX 7.1: A Casting Breakdown for Performance Capture**

| | |
|---|---|
| PROJECT RADON<br>PROD COMPANY: NEW DIMENSIONS GAMES<br>VIDEO GAME: SAG/AFTRA<br>MAJOR FRANCHISE | Director: Tom Keegan<br>Casting Dir: Karina Bergman<br>START: mid-May plus additional shoots<br>LOCATION: Los Angeles<br>karinabergmancast@gmail.com |

SUBMISSIONS DUE BY MARCH 15TH. SEND DEMO REELS AND PLEASE NOTE IF ARTIST HAS PERFORMANCE CAPTURE EXPERIENCE.

ALL ROLES REQUIRE ON-CAMERA AUDITIONS FOR PERFORMANCE CAPTURE. NO LIKENESS

APPROX. RATES MINIMUM 2x-3x scale plus 10% agency fees.

**Lead Roles**

**Lance**

Male. 30s. Bi-racial or Multi-racial, American accent. Relaxed confidence, grounded demeanor. Speaks with a straightforward but careful manner. Weighs every word. Veteran interplanetary fighter who is weary of war but will never give up the struggle. Works to end conflict by winning. Leading man. Tall, broad-shouldered, athletic. Bi-racial or Multi-racial, American accent.

**Arjun**

Male. Mid 40s. South Asian with Delhi accent.

Good humored and wise. A talented navigator, he also has a strongly tuned intuition and receives messages and impulses he believes to be from guiding entities. He carries himself with the confidence and fluid poise of a dancer. Arjun is willing to go with the flow, whether winning or losing. WILL BE COACHED TO SPEAK SOME DIALOGUE IN AN INVENTED LANGUAGE

**Sekh**

Female. 50s. Any ethnicity.

A large and powerful queen with a fierce warrior code: strength, glory and justice above all. Politically savvy, she can be confrontative and menacing, but also a skilled negotiator at the table. Stands for the rights of her people, first and foremost. She has seen politicians and leaders rise and fall so takes nothing as a given. 6' or taller. MUST HAVE STUNT OR WEAPONS HANDLING ABILITIES.

PROJECT RADON IS A SCIENCE FICTION ACTION-ADVENTURE GAME.

### *After the Breakdown*

Creating the breakdown is just the beginning but an important part of the process. Think of your breakdown as the cover letter you send with a resume. It introduces your project, establishes its credentials, and attracts interested buyers. Take the time to do it properly and review it as carefully as you would when applying for a job. It's a marketing piece for the project.

Once complete, breakdowns are sent to agents, managers, and, in some markets, directly to actors by listing them on casting services. In the bigger markets, this is done through Breakdown Express or, in the UK, Spotlight. After receiving the breakdown, agents and interested parties will submit headshots, demo reels, self-tapes, and other materials from their clients. Either the casting director, development team, or director then makes lists of actors to see, and auditions are scheduled.

### How to Work with a Casting Director

Casting is a time-consuming and nuanced process, which is why I now mostly work with a casting director, especially for pcap. There are numerous good reasons to work with one. They have solid relationships within the talent world and can open doors for your project. Casting directors know which actors are solid workers and can direct you toward the really good ones while steering you away from folks who are either problematic, or who might be very involved in other projects that will be difficult to schedule around. They can also clue you in on up-and-coming talent who might be very good but are new on the scene.

My casting director prescreens all of the pcap submissions and makes lists. She might ask me if I'm interested in a certain actor or if there are any that I'm already thinking of for the role. If there are new people she wants to try out, she will audition them and show me the recordings. In this way, she not only shows me the talent, but by gauging how I respond, she gets a good idea of how I'm thinking about the role. She will also make a list of higher-profile people I might want to see, and those folks will usually come straight to the director without a first audition. When we get to the callback audition stage, she and her team will schedule all of that and make sure the director, the actors, and their teams have the necessary materials and information. After the casting is done, the casting director may coordinate the deal making, the actors' schedules, the payment information, and even getting the contracts signed before handing everything over to the production team.

Sometimes, a talent coordinator or audio director makes the initial approach to agents. A director can also cast through demos, but there really is no substitute for having the actor actually read for the role. Demos are carefully constructed talent showcase pieces, but to find out what it's like to work with a particular actor, you need experience with them. At the end of this phase, final callbacks are held in person or live online.

For voiceover casting, the process is a little bit different. Voiceover actors, through their agents or directly, submit self-recorded auditions from **sides,** or short snippets from the working script of the project. In the voiceover world, the breakdown usually contains these audition sides. It all goes out as one package to voice agents, who solicit recorded reads from their actors and return a set of auditions to the team. While it's rare these days, I've also had live VO callbacks in the booth.

Some game developers just want to see the recorded auditions, and some want to be part of the process. At the very least, whoever will be directing the actors should be present. Callbacks are a valuable opportunity for a performance director to develop a relationship with an actor around the material. Whatever ground is laid in the callback can be further developed during production.

### Audition Sides

I like to have at least two short scenes for every character. Each scene should be no more than two pages. The audition scenes should just be a way to get a take on what the actor does with the scene, and whether they can take direction. It's not critical that the scenes even appear in the game. What's most important is that the audition material shows the range the actor needs to have for the role. For one game, I received audition materials from the developer for a voice role that just consisted of radio navigation lines. After I had already cast the actor, I found out the role also required a death scene on the battlefield! Fortunately, the actor pulled it off, but it could have been a costly mistake if they couldn't have acted a convincing death scene.

Remember that game scripts are often in spreadsheet form. I have many times been given lists of lines in a spreadsheet as a script, with no information as to whether these lines are a monologue, standalone prompts to the player, or one side of a conversation. I know many actors who have been in the same situation. If it's a conversation, *give the lines in-between as well*; if you only give an individual character's lines, the actor will have to guess what just happened. As much as possible without giving plot points away, give some sense of the Place, Time, Action, even if you have to make it up.

### *Translation*

If the script calls for an actor to speak in a language other than your local language, make sure the script is translated. Asking an actor to translate on the spot is not only highly unprofessional, but it takes a large portion of the actor's attention just to translate—attention that could better be put to the actor's performance.

### *Security*

Security is critical with casting materials. I had once had an entire project leaked online. Back in the days of ftp sites, one particular talent agency took its security down briefly to update software. Soon after that, I found a piece of copy online with notes to the actors in my handwriting and an entire article devoted to (mostly incorrect) assumptions about the game. The producers threatened to sue me, until it was pointed out that all the other publishers also had their audition sides posted on sites for actors to access, and that a leak could happen to any one of them. Nevertheless, I was ready to go out and hunt down this hacker to put them out of their misery.

It's tricky to scrub casting material of too much identifying information, but it's a good practice. I usually create a dummy project similar to the one we're working on, but with changed circumstances. For example, when casting *Wolfenstein: The New Order*, I created a game that was a Bourne-style European action piece set in the 1960s. The circumstances and emotional relationships were the same; the time period was the only difference. Even with a high level of security, give the actors context for the scene. If the scene is a spoiler for something in the game, it's probably not the one to use for auditions.

Make sure to fill the actor in on PTA details—Place, Time, Action. (Figure 7.2)

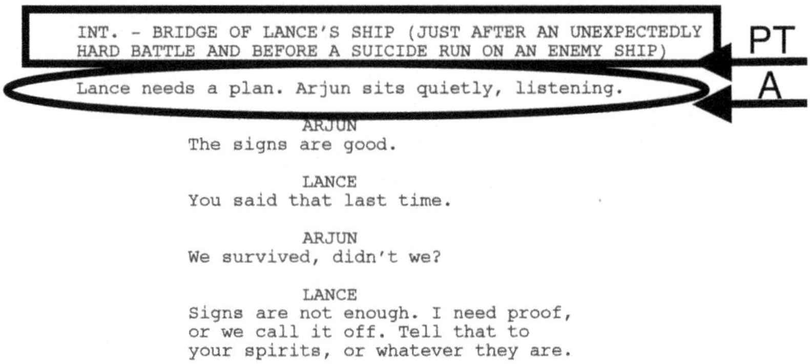

INT. - BRIDGE OF LANCE'S SHIP (JUST AFTER AN UNEXPECTEDLY HARD BATTLE AND BEFORE A SUICIDE RUN ON AN ENEMY SHIP)

Lance needs a plan. Arjun sits quietly, listening.

ARJUN
The signs are good.

LANCE
You said that last time.

ARJUN
We survived, didn't we?

LANCE
Signs are not enough. I need proof, or we call it off. Tell that to your spirits, or whatever they are.



**Figure 7.2** Audition "sides" with place, time, and action called out.

## The Audition Process

Cast early. You need time to develop the materials, and once posted, at least a week or more for agents to submit. Scheduling auditions takes time, and holding them on more than one day gives actors options. It takes a team to run callback or live auditions, even if online. Casting directors or assistants make sure actors have the most recent scripts and any other information they need. In a live audition with an actor, director, and developers, both sides of the table are checking each other out. It's often a loose first rehearsal for the actor who will get the job. Whether you are an observer or you are running the audition, do not eat, check your phone, answer emails, or allow yourself in any way to get distracted while the actor is working. Give the actors your full attention and respect. If you can't do that, don't attend.

### *In the Room*

When the actor arrives, welcome them and introduce everyone who is there. Don't just show them where to stand. As a director, you are responsible for creating an environment for them to be comfortable enough to do their best work. You may be seeing this person a lot as a co-worker.

Devise a casting process that reveals everything you need to know about the actor. In most of my auditions for performance capture, after the actor says their name, they show both profiles in a full body shot. In industry parlance, this is called a **slate**. Then, I ask them to walk around the space in character. In the 1970s, the visionary British director Peter Brook took a troupe of actors through Africa to explore the essence of theater with audiences who had no concept of theater. After some success and failures, the director and troupe came to find one universal gesture: walking. Watching an actor walk in character tells so much, especially in a medium where movement and gesture are king. Someone who walks like a ballet dancer will never be mistaken for a soldier, just as someone who slouches and slumps across a space will never convincingly portray a parkour runner. Their body language just says otherwise.

Some actors don't take the slate or character walk seriously. They are nervous or feel degraded by having to show their profile. Transparency is key to making the actor feel at home. Explain to the actor that if they get the job, the animators will need to begin tweaking the character to fit on their body frame, and their movements will become the character's. The actors who are cast will have to trust their director. Begin to build that trust in the audition.

Ask them if they have questions about the material, and fill in any missing details that may not have been apparent from what they were sent. Tell them a little about the game. If the scenes have been disguised for security purposes, if they have signed an NDA (non-disclosure agreement) fill them in on the real circumstances. Too many times, when I have explained the real circumstances, actors have said, "Oh, I thought it was something different. Can I just show you what I practiced?" Right off, this actor is most likely out of the running. If they cannot adjust to changed circumstances, they are probably not flexible enough to work in performance-capture on a game.

After discussing details, give actors a chance to show what they have prepared. Even if they have perfectly captured what you are looking for, give them an adjustment. Try the scene a different way so you can see how the actor adjusts. Think of the audition as an exploration, not a finished product.

The British actor and director David Harewood came to our casting in London for *Battlefield 3*. He was a rising star, known in the UK, but as an American, I was not familiar with his work. He caused a stir among the Brits when he came into the building. He was extremely casual, riding up on a bicycle and entering the casting room. “Let’s do some work, shall we?” he said. “What are your ideas for this material? How would you like to try it out?” He embodied the creative flexibility and willingness I admire in actors. He got the role and I used him in several other games. Not insignificantly, he was also a gamer who appreciated the intricacy and power of interactive storytelling.

**BOX 7.2: Recipe for Pcap Auditions**

1. **Slate**. The actor says their name, height, and turns in profile.
2. **Character walk** across the space, possibly with a slight run.
3. **Movement improvisation** with a prop weapon if the role calls for it.
4. **Scene set-up**. Invite questions. Discuss the previous moment. Describe the blocking, and the environment.
5. **Scene**. The actor performs what they have prepared.
6. **Adjustments** and comments.
7. **Voice**. Often, I will hand the actor a few in-game lines, battle shouts, etc. to see their vocal range.
8. **Thank you** for coming today!

There are limits to how many times an actor can be asked to audition. According to union rules and generally accepted procedures, directors can get a reading or audition and one free callback. Many actors will agree to a second callback or “chemistry read” if they are in the final running for the role. After that, producers may have to pay to bring an actor in again. Paid callbacks are more common in the EU and the UK.

### Making Selections

Making selections from casting can be an overwhelming prospect. On-camera pcap auditions can bring in hundreds and hundreds of submissions. For voiceover, a single role can bring in thousands of recorded voice auditions, many from highly qualified candidates.

How do you pick and choose who gets on the shortlist and who eventually gets cast?

Even with shortlists, there is an art to reviewing auditions. From personal experience, I can tell you that order bias is one of the most difficult challenges to overcome. The first 25 people all seem like interesting possibilities. Then you start to get choosier. You start feeling like, "seen that, seen that…" and start looking for something fresh, something that stands out to you. Yet, it is the reviewer who is not fresh, and the people who got their auditions in first are in a better place in the pool. Then, toward the end of the process, you get that last minute person who blows everybody out of the water, but only because you've seen the same thing over and over for days. You could have missed someone really good because they weren't different enough from the person who came before them. Just like looking at color swatches or listening to sounds, they will appear very different depending on whom came before or after them.

My personal way to combat this is to start at the beginning, review and rank choices, stop before you get tired and then go to the last submissions, work backward, jump to the middle, etc. The idea is to break up the odds that the people who got in early don't dominate the field.

### Hiring the Actor

Once you've decided who you want to cast, the next step has to be handled carefully. Directors and developers should keep in mind that they are not just hiring an acting machine. They are hiring a person. A qualified gate-keeper should be the first point of contact. This is usually a casting director, talent coordinator, performance director, or audio specialist. They have some experience interacting with the world of actors and their representatives and won't make the kind of mistakes less-informed people can easily fall into. What are those mistakes?

Let's say you have a script in hand, and you have your dream cast in mind. You look online for some contact information about an actor whose work you've admired. You eventually get in touch with their agent or attorney, and say, "We're working on a videogame and want to hire this special actor. We're huge fans and would love to work with them. How much do they cost?" Do this, and you can be sure you will either have the door slammed in your face or you will be taken to the cleaners.

Here's a reality about videogames: they might be high on the actors' list of jobs they would like to get, but games are at the bottom of the priority list for agents and managers. Part of this is because games are newer outlets and the actor's team is less familiar with how they work. It's also because their payment, while fairly robust up front, has no back-end or residual structure for the management to profit from in the future. Agents get only 10% of an actor's pay, while managers can get up to 25%. (In the US, these rules are set by law.) So, for an agent to turn a profit, they need the pay to go up exponentially. For higher profile actors, their lawyer or publicist gets a cut as well. After taxes, the actor is lucky to get 50% of the money they are earning at the session.

The "low status" of videogames works against developers in scheduling as well. For pcap, make sure it is written into the deal that once the dates for the shoot are set, your production is in "first position." This means they must tell other productions those dates are not available. A strong deal memo, the written form of a pre-contract that spells out the important points of the agreement, can prevent problems and misunderstandings down the line. There is nothing worse than starting down the road with a performer who then gets another production that conflicts with yours. If your production is not in first position, you will have very little leverage when it comes to securing the actor for the recording dates.

Always have at least three choices for every role. Things change quickly in the entertainment industry, and an actor who seems like a sure thing might fall out at the last moment. When production is pressed for time and doesn't have interesting backup choices, they are in a weak position when it comes to negotiating the points of a deal.

It's a good idea to separate the creative team from the deal makers. This is where your casting director and a paralegal or attorney can be helpful. The posturing, cringe-inducing demands, and horse-trading can create an illusory gulf between a performer and the team. More than once I've been the chief negotiator as well as the performance director and I've had to work hard not hold a grudge against an actor whose reps have put me through hell to get them there. Most of the time, the actor has no idea of how the negotiating has gone down behind the scenes. Leave the deal-making to the professionals and focus on preparing to direct the fine talent you are about to welcome to your world as collaborators and colleagues.

## References

*Battlefield 3.* Developed by DICE, Electronic Arts, 2011.
*Breakdown Services, Ltd.* "Breakdown Express." *Breakdown Services*, www.breakdownexpress.com
Heilpern, John. *Conference of the Birds: The Story of Peter Brook in Africa.* Faber & Faber, 1977.
*Indiana Jones and the Great Circle.* Developed by MachineGames, published by Bethesda Softworks, 2024. © & ™ 2024 Lucasfilm Ltd. All rights reserved.
"Spotlight." *Spotlight*, 2024, www.spotlight.com

# 8
# Workshop and Rehearsal

**In This Chapter**

- How workshop can benefit a production
- Giving script notes
- How to conduct a table read
- Previsualization and blocking
- The importance of rehearsal

I'm in rehearsal room with a small group of actors, preparing for the **vertical slice** of a gritty, realistic, military shooter game. The vertical slice is a small sample "proof of concept" portion of a game that has been given a tentative green light. It shows that the team has the technology, the talent, and the production capacity to make the game and ship it on time.

The producer and writer of our game have stressed its "realism," and we've cast accordingly. Instead of the bourbon growl of drill-sergeant voices, we've cast typical American-sounding men who in civilian life might be a teacher or the owners of a shop. A large part of the dialogue is radio chatter, and I want the squad to have the feeling that they are a cohesive unit.

As a rehearsal technique, I come up with the idea to ask the actors to have a conversation about lunch and then launch into the military talk. My theory is that instead of sounding like cliché military grunts, the squad will sound like co-workers, people who've come to view life-and-death matters as routine when not under fire. The improv works beautifully, and the actors start to build an interesting rapport with each other.

At the break, the audio director, who I've met for the first time today, pulls me aside. "What are you doing? What's with this lunchtime talk?

 DOI: 10.1201/9781003558910-9

My nephew is in Special Forces, and I called him just now. He says they would never talk like that on a secure channel. NEVER!"

I keep my cool and explain that the improv is a rehearsal technique. I reassure him that players would never hear the pre-roll. They would only hear the lines. The audio director is not satisfied. As the production rolls on, he questions everything I do and say. He is even keeping a notebook of phrases he's heard me use to prompt the actors as evidence that I'm unqualified to direct this production.

What he didn't know was that *in the imagination game of directing actors, there doesn't need to be any obvious connection between the prompt and the result.* The connection comes from the relationship the director has with the actor. If I had to do a scene where I was paralyzed with fear, a director who knew my history could say to me, "Report card… sewer" knowing I once lost my report card in a sewer on my way to school. But sometimes, the people you work for are not accustomed to the unique ways directors and actors create performances. As it turns out, I'm not hired back for the main game, and I'm just as glad because I can't do my best work when I don't have the support of the whole team.

Around the same time, the Oscar-nominated documentary *Restrepo* is released to great acclaim. *Restrepo* is about a group of American soldiers in Afghanistan, fighting together in one of the most dangerous places on earth, the Korengal "Valley of Death." In one scene, a soldier is setting up a.50cal weapon high on a mountain. As he sets up the machine-gun nest, he has a casual walkie-talkie chat with a fellow soldier. What do they discuss? A recent trip home, a ranch, animals … exactly the "casual mood under dangerous circumstances" I was going for. So maybe it's not true that soldiers NEVER have small talk over the radio.

After watching *Restrepo*, I couldn't get my mind off the vertical slice I'd been working on, and how rehearsal was leading us in the right direction. It was, as rehearsals must be, a process of discovering the best we had to give. In videogames, as in theater, if you skip the trial-and-error process of rehearsal, success is a hit-or-miss proposition. And with the amount of effort and expense it takes to make a videogame, hit-or-miss is not where you want to be.

My team and I have developed a set of steps we call "Workshop," a multi-step process that builds in time for examining the script, getting it on its feet, and giving the actors and directors time to probe the material. Workshop can be a great term to describe the director's homework as well.

What we are about to lay out to you as workshop is an ideal way to develop and explore the subtext of game cinematics and its execution. When I worked in television, no script or series would ever be greenlit without extensive notes from producers, development execs, and directors. (Even so, many stinkers still get into the pipeline.) Star actors and directors may say, "I don't rehearse," but somewhere along the line, rehearsals are happening. Camera rehearsals and lighting rehearsals are made possible with the use of stand-ins who look very similar to the actor and sometimes even shoot the scene if they are only seen from the back. The first filmed takes then become rehearsals for the principal actors.

In many circumstances, you are not afforded the time or access to hold a complete workshop. You are working with an undigested script that the actors only got the night before and needs to be rewritten on the fly. You may have to "shoot the rehearsal." For voiceover, it's highly likely you haven't even seen the script before you sat down in the booth.

But by considering Workshop and all its steps, at least you will know in your mind how to properly prepare a project for shooting and recording. As a director, you can lead the charge. You can suggest workshop procedures and show your producers and the development team how much benefit comes from them. You will know what to ask for to do your best work. Your team will thank you and your actors will thank you. And ultimately, your players will thank you.

A reminder from your friendly neighborhood performance director: Finding the three big facts—**PTA**—is an excellent jumping-off point for discussion at every stage, for these questions quickly reveal holes in the overall narrative and each scene in particular.

1. Where are we physically? (Place in physical space—P)
2. What just happened? (Location in narrative time—T)
3. What is the action? (Current action to play—A)

### Workshop

Workshop is pre-shoot and usually involves the director and the development team. Sometimes a lead actor might be present if he or she is heavily invested in the narrative and a strong collaborator. The point of Workshop is not to *nail down* the narrative. The goal is to make sure that the narrative has been carefully examined from many different sides before going into the costly-yet-exciting mocap volume with costly-yet-exciting actors. Workshop includes all of the following elements:

- Script notes
- Director's vision
- Previs
- Blocking
- Table read and review of casting
- Rehearsal

#### *Script Notes*

For me, my own first reading of a script is a precious moment. Never again will I, as the director, be able to see the material with the fresh eyes that a player will have on first encounter. So I take careful notes on my questions, ideas, and responses to scenes and lines in the script. I ignore these first impressions at my peril.

I recently worked on a game that had tremendous potential, with a very open team who really listened to my notes and suggestions. At the beginning of our work, I noticed glaring inconsistencies in the script. Some of these were addressed early on, but soon fell out of sight with all the work and intricacies of getting the script ready for shooting. It's easy to lose sight of problems because a director often falls in love with the script and the cast and the team. When this game came out, the early inconsistencies I had originally pointed out were pounced on mercilessly by reviewers. I wished I had kept these problems in mind so they could have been fixed before the launch.

You might be working with teams and writers who are resistant to director's notes. It takes a gentle and supportive hand to guide script development if team members are attached to what has been written. Nevertheless, a director should always have those notes, along with a handful of ideas that are solutions to the weaknesses.

Script notes can be incredibly helpful to writers and developers, especially if the director has an experienced eye for how to structure a scene. You stumble across a scene that is chock full of player direction but has little to no dramatic conflict or tension. Then later in the script you might see the same stuff reoccur without any dramatic development or change. These instances need a director's attention.

I evaluate the script on its own merits. I'm always on the lookout for answers to particular dramatic questions:

- What story are the developers trying to tell?
- What will be happening visually, sonically, and kinesthetically?
- What gameplay comes before and after the narrative scene?
- What are the characters' actions, and are they different enough to articulate?
- What is the emotional moment or climax of the scene?
- Does the dramatic set-up serve what the developers are trying to accomplish?

Go beyond "I like it/I don't like it" and give only actionable feedback. It's easy to criticize the work someone has done on a piece, but what is the basis of your criticism and how can the writers and developers make it better? When giving feedback, articulate the themes of the script/story/treatment, and reflect on how the scenes support or detract from those themes. Even if the work is poorly constructed from a dramatic perspective—and deserves criticism—honor the work that was done by the team in your script notes.

In workshop meetings and storyboard discussions, the director can lay the early groundwork for how the subtext works in the scene, what actions the characters are playing, and where the climax of the scene occurs. Subtext is challenging and highly personal. Expecting other team members to intuitively have the same subtextual ideas is a recipe for conflict down the line, on-set or in post-production. Articulating those ideas to your collaborators—not as demands but as a loose mapping of the character arcs—is respectful and builds trust.

### *The Table Read*

The table read is an exciting moment in the development of any project. The actors who have been cast are brought to the table, the development team and key stakeholders are assembled and hungry, and the script is served up, ready to be carved and eaten. The table read may be the only time this entire cast is together. There is a freshness and liveliness to the experience. Not only is this about the script, it's also very largely about *connection*. Unless they have already met, the players are getting a better sense of each other and the development team. They want to meet their collaborators. Everyone is nervous and excited (Figure 8.1).

**Figure 8.1** A table read with actor Victoria Atkin, the author, writer Zach Betka, and actor Elizabeth Grullon. (Photo by Katja Kulenkampff.)

As with all experiences where anticipation is riding high, disappointment may also be right around the corner. Most actors will attempt to bring the script alive, but some may choose to read in a monotone, with little or no expression. *Don't panic and recast based on a table read!* A table read is not a way to confirm casting choices. If it's a chemistry read to find out whether actors have a natural spark between them, it should be labeled as such in advance. What's important in a table read is that the producers and the director set a tone of exploration and permission. Listen for sparks and connections. For the director and the developers, the table read is the only other time they can encounter the script with fresh eyes.

For serious working actors, the table read is part of a process that involves reading and listening and may be a first encounter with the words out loud. If an actor is of such stature that they do not audition and then deliver a flat read at the table, it can be jarring for the producers. Communication about expectations can solve this. If an actor is expected to try out some choices or deliver a performance, that expectation should be conveyed beforehand in a sensitive way by the director or producer. Language such as, "Let's try X for the character in the read today" or "keep the pace crisp by picking up the cues" is enough to anchor the actor. As with any direction, actionable adjustments allow the artist to remain in creative control of their performance while serving the needs of the production.

*Previs*

Previs is entertainment industry shorthand for the previsualization. Previs is a virtual pre-production rehearsal for the digital and special-effects scenes in a game or film. With such a heavy reliance on storytelling that is mainly produced in post-production, it's vital that scenes be imagined in advance and tried out before put into the production pipeline. It becomes very expensive to correct a mistake in post-production that could have been solved beforehand with proper planning. Previs can be anything from a stop-action animation slide show called an *animatic*, made from a storyboard and set to music or voices, to a fully resolved 3D motion capture scene which can be set between elements of game play. Especially for a game, where all the elements must go into the game engine and eventually work together seamlessly, low-tech and high-tech previs help the developers plan what they need to do to keep their vision on budget and on schedule.

I once saw a presentation on the 2016 live action film, *The Jungle Book*. A delightful scene—with Bill Murray playing Baloo, and the young actor Neel Sethi playing Mowgli—was completely previsualized on a giant turntable with motion capture actors, so that precious set time with a child actor and a demanding movie star was kept to a minimum.

For the director and game team, previs often starts with sharing of environments, gameplay mechanics, floor diagrams, sets, and other key components of an upcoming mocap shoot or voice recording. They might produce a rough animatic showing how the characters will be positioned and what they will likely be seeing. The animatic can show how much time an explosion or magical effect will take and how long the actors have to imagine responding to it.

In a *Star Wars* game, for example, a previs animatic would show a character in the cockpit of a ship, flipping switches, steering through an asteroid field, and seeing an attack on an outlying planet. It's helpful to show these rough previses to actors who will be in a VO booth or on a mocap set with limited visuals. A well-prepared director will always give an actor a prompt, an image, or a previs to respond to. Just remember not to dictate the response!

### *Blocking*

**Blocking** is the grouping and movement of people through the scene. In theater, blocking revolves around creating stage pictures and focusing the audience's attention. In film, blocking is all about the movement of people in the frame, or the movement of the actors and the camera. In a game, blocking may be some combination of both. For example, in a movie-like cinematic, the player is usually "locked," meaning they can't interact with the scene until it's over. Once the player is free to "roam" around the environment, it is sometimes necessary to keep the game moving by placing a character somewhere in the space to force a confrontation, or sometimes keep the player from going through a doorway too early, or even prevent the player from going back to where they have just come from.

One of the remarkable things about digital cinematography in a virtual environment like a videogame is that the "camera" can literally move through walls. The virtual camera, or **VCam,** is a digital eye, so to speak. Like a camera, it has selectable lens settings for focal length, focus distance, and aperture. The operator moves that eye around the virtual environment and captures shots that can be edited together in a cinematic. Nothing is being captured optically except as a video reference for the artists who will turn the mocap data into a scene in post-production. I have blocked scenes in performance capture as if I was staging a play, with the audience on all side, with room for a camera to be placed afterwards by a cinematics team. I have staged scenes with long tracking shots monitored by a technician with a handheld virtual camera, and

I have also shot performance capture with a multi-camera setup designed by the cinematographer. In the latter, the mocap scene is also shot on video with long lenses to show a cinematic intention which will be used by the cinematics team to recreate the rendered 3D footage virtually in the game. (No matter what kind of virtual camera is being employed for the scene, the live shoot is always also recorded on video for reference.)

For a performance director, blocking has so many elements that subtext often becomes an afterthought. Time after time I've seen a storyboard or cinematic concept fall flat when staged because it wasn't based on subtext. This is another reason why directors do their script analysis in advance. Blocking takes time and experimentation if based on subtext instead of pictures and compositions. We develop the blocking in Workshop because otherwise, it can take up all of our rehearsal time, leaving nothing for performance exploration.

There are many directors who tightly pre-plan their blocking, before an actor even steps on the stage. While this might be necessary for heavily cinematic productions with multiple camera moves, the practice can run the risk of eliminating any opportunity for subtext to inform the blocking.

Planning is important, but keep it loose with options. I try to find a happy medium between strict planning and total freedom: I like a floor map that shows where in the environment the actor comes in, where the cinematic team expects the main action to take place, and where the character exits or faces when the cinematic ends. But between those spots, I wait to see what movements *naturally* occur based on the subtext. Stage directions in the script might work, but unless they line up with the subtext, they will read as false or stagey.

A **blocking rehearsal** is a trial run for a director to see how humans might move with these words in space, usually before the actual actors get into the volume. I have done blocking rehearsals with staff members, animators, actors and stunt people, or a mix. Before blocking rehearsal begins, I've also used dolls, pencils, and coins while doing all of the voices. Storyboards often confound me, but by recreating them with toy figurines, I come to my own understanding of what the storyboard artist is trying to do.

A sense of freedom and play is a fantastic asset when trying out early blocking. Blocking rehearsals give a director and a team good ideas for how to stage the scene while allowing the subtext to guide the movements of the characters. Yet nothing should be completely locked down until the *actual* actors have their go at it. There's something very raw about the first time scripted words are spoken out loud by bodies in space. Sometimes, scenes work immediately, but usually, they're awkward. Working through the awkwardness takes the scene right into the subtext. Where does the character *naturally* want to go? What do they *really* want to say in this situation? The director doesn't have to figure it all out. Ask the actors or staff or whoever is in the scene what *they* would do in this situation. What is *their* instinct? Is what they are saying really necessary, or can a gesture or tone of voice convey it?

One afternoon when I was in Suzanne Shepherd's Meisner acting class, there was a scene between a mother and a daughter. The mother had to give the daughter a precious object, but when she handed it to the daughter, the mother held on to the object a little too long. She couldn't let go. Suzanne leaped up and said, "There it is! That's the subtext right there in this gesture. This could be the poster for the show, right here. Always let the blocking come out of the subtext."

Pause and let that sink in: *Always let the blocking come out of the subtext.*

The late French Canadian director Jean-Marc Valée preferred to work this way, especially on his HBO show *Sharp Objects*. There were no storyboards or shot lists used in making the show because he preferred to allow the actors to express themselves. In an interview he said, "I'm reacting to what they're doing, instead of being active and telling them what I'll do with the camera," he said, adding: "I love it. You know, I'm like a kid on a set, a kid playing with a huge toy and having fun." Yet sometimes it is necessary to loosely block a scene in advance if there are complex elements that would eat up time in production. This is where your work with stand-ins, staff members, or dolls, is useful.

In *Jedi: Survivor*, the reunion scene where Cal (the player) and his crew reunite with Cal's former mentor, Cere, has a number of different beats. Cere is at her computing station at the top of the scene. Cal, the player, is free to enter into the room or walk around, but once he gets close to Cere, the **cinematic**—during which the player no longer has control over the action—launches, and Cal has an emotionally complex talk with Cere at her station. In the next beat of the scene, the other four members of the crew join, each with their own unique backstory with Cere. The scene has a feeling of the band reuniting, like a family or tribe, where fractures and competing agendas are right below the surface.

So, how did I block this complex scene? With six performers having face cams, body data, and voice, there was always the risk of a technical meltdown from too much data. We also wanted to avoid unnecessary editing cuts to keep post-production costs from going over budget. So we decided to shoot the Cal/Cere scene in a separate shot, and then block the reunion to be shot all the way through in one take.

*Running as much of the scene as possible without a cut eases the post-production team's work and expense.* One challenge, though, is that the more people and the longer the scene, the more likely something will go wrong and we'll have to reshoot the scene again from the top. So the performance director—especially when working with a multi-camera cinematic setup—has to carefully rehearse and then choreograph the scene along with the camera moves to make sure that the single take will work. Workshop is the place to make these discoveries. Blocking through subtext, followed by thoughtful rehearsal and refinement, are critical to creating a complex scene that is efficient and impactful.

In the sinking car scene at the opening of *Battlefield 4*, four men are trapped in a car. The captain is mortally wounded and he knows it. The scene is first-person, meaning the player is the camera and will only be seen as a pair of arms within the frame. The blocking was tight because of the small space. The captain had to be near the player because the cinematic turns into an interactive event where the player must take the captain's gun and shoot the window out for the squad to escape and survive. Not a lot of walking around in the blocking, but plenty of body movement such as head turns and pounding on the windows and doors of the vehicle.

In a first-person scene like this, where *the player's character is the camera*, the director is not necessarily relying on a camera angle or cut to tell the story. Rather, we are creating an environment in which drama occurs. In first-person perspective scenes, other characters may have to respond to the player-character, who may or may not be at a given position in the room. Again, it's important that we're trying this out during Workshop: Why leave complex problem-solving like this to the last minute, when you have a roomful of expensive actors in mocap suits? Will the doors open in or out? Is there a handle or switch the player must use? When all of these technical problems are solved in workshop, there is more time and energy for the actors to play and flesh out their subtext, instead of figuring out how a door works.

### Rehearsal

The importance of rehearsal for performance capture cannot be overstated. The stakes are high, but there is still room to noodle around. In a perfect world, everyone has done their homework. The director has a plan for the scenes, the team has all the **assets**—the props and sets—ready for rehearsal, and the actors have been investigating the script, which they received well in advance.

Let the cast do a quick read-through, then address their questions about the scenes. Give them any props, weapons, or costume pieces they must work with, and show them around the set and environment. Encourage the actors to explore—to sit in the chairs, to open and touch the doors and surfaces. A director can glean new information and ideas just by watching people interact naturally in a space.

Next, walk the actors through any blocking you have already decided on, but be open to their ideas and suggestions. Where is their impulse to move and speak? Hold the blocking and stage directions lightly. Let them improvise any beats that are not working. If lines feel forced or awkward, ask the actors to suggest changes, and run them by the writers or the team. Get the scene on its feet and working but leave room for it to cook. Keep the tone creative and exploratory. Keep an open mind as the actors develop their performances. Of course, you and the team have a vision for the scene, and it's your job to skillfully steer your collaborators toward this vision. But allow the vision to shift and change if something better arises.

The urge to nail the scene, to squeeze the performance out of the actors, is deeply ingrained. As I write this, I'm on a break during a rehearsal day with 12 actors. The pressure of dealing with a crowd, with multiple mini-scenes intersecting at key points, has been like wrestling a Rubik's Cube larger than my head. Now that we are on a break, it's occurred to me that I've fallen into the trap of trying to get full-on performances during a rehearsal instead of taking the attitude of exploration, the "probe."

With blocking solved in advance, rehearsals are a time for actors to explore without the pressure of having to deliver a finished performance. Rehearsal can include an improvisation for an off-camera scene that might have been significant for a relationship between characters, a run of a scene done the "wrong" way to energize static or uninspired performances, or a gradual process where actors do the scene in their own words and gradually feed in the lines as written.

Rehearsals can also be used to swap personal stories that ground the events of the scene in real experience, or to do the Meisner "repeating game," where actors repeat each other's lines in a similar intonation before speaking their own line. This exercise builds in a strong sense of listening and "realness" to a conversation that breaks through any mere illustrating of the lines. (Figure 8.2).

**Figure 8.2** Rehearsal shot with Debra Wilson, Victoria Atkin, T.J. Ramini, and the author. Gesture is important in performance-capture scenes. (Photo by Katja Kulenkampff.)

For example, the Russians in *Battlefield 3* are on a life-or-death mission near the end of their career as mercenaries. Their banter references a long and roguish history together. So we improvised scenes from their past for rehearsal purposes. Once they had improvised an imaginary shared history, the actors could come to the scene already carrying a relationship beyond the written word.

Often, when rehearsing and exploring scenes, after a read through, I will ask actors to improvise the scene in their own words. This helps them make the scene their own. The natural chemistry between the performers comes through. Some actors may find this difficult, but with encouragement to feel completely free, even forbidden to use any of the actual text, they can find life in the scene. The second stage might be to mix their own words with some of the text. Finally, ask them to speak only in the text but keeping the energy they found with their own words.

This comes back to our rule about not illustrating the text, which hamstrings so many actors. It's not only illustrating the *text* that's crippling, but also the *action* written between the text. Actions that are key to the plot or character often fall flat when not felt as spontaneous.

The process of finding the words from improvisation is essential for Shakespeare or period pieces, which might suffer from a frightful stiffness due to the respect afforded to high or low status period work. The best films, TV shows, plays or games set in period times always make the period feel contemporary, despite the different rules of dress, language or behavior. Once, in a dream, I was transported to a medieval village. To my surprise, it felt as real as today, only with different clothes and antiquated technology. The same need to conduct business, gossip, and find one's way across town felt excruciatingly familiar, as real as now.

It's easier for the actor to memorize lines if they have a relationship to the material and to the action of the scene. In rehearsal, an actor can find the full extent of the arc or breadth of their character by trying out a variety of scenes that will be shot on different days, so that every scene contains the full character who will go through various situations.

I like to rehearse two days of shooting material in one rehearsal day. Sometimes, I even have less time and more material to cram into a rehearsal day, and as a director I feel frantic with how much I need to accomplish. The wonderful thing about rehearsals is that they don't have to look a certain way. There's an art to balancing the many vital needs for the shoot with the spirit of discovery and play. Rehearsals are a preparatory activity for a performance, *not* a performance itself. It's a big mistake to judge a rehearsal as a performance. I've had worried calls from producers and team members who are frantic at the state of an actor's work at rehearsal. Of course, they have the right to be concerned if there are warning signs that the actor has been miscast or is not up to the job. But in my experience, miscasting is rare. It's more often the case that a producer is looking at a rehearsal as if it is the final performance.

To see the extent to which rehearsal performances can differ from final performances, watch clips of casting tapes of famous actors auditioning for iconic roles and watch videos of films before sound effects and **ADR/walla** (background conversation and noise) are added. They seem flat and unconvincing, diamonds in the rough. Often, performers are "saving it" for the real moment of shooting or performing, knowing they only have so much emotional energy in reserve to spend on a particular scene. Even first takes in shooting can seem this way, but once an actor works up to performance level, with the help of good direction, the difference can be nothing short of miraculous.

True, some directors like to "shoot the rehearsal"—which means not rehearsing at all—and there is a magic to an in-the-moment, discovered performance. While the sudden beauty of discovery in rehearsal is wonderful, it may not be moving in the right direction. The director's job is much larger than capturing raw magic. Rest assured; you'll fall in love with certain things during rehearsal that do not fit the needs of the work as a whole. This is where you must be willing to "kill your darlings." The director has to chart the movement of the relationships in the scenes and the character arcs over the whole of the piece. This is why I like to find magic in rehearsal, when the stakes are lower, and then *let it cook* for a day or so before, after careful consideration, we lay it down in performance.

I recently had a conversation with a performance director who liked to rehearse in the morning and shoot in the afternoon. I asked them whether they felt the actors had time to really integrate the rehearsal.

The director answered that the actors were very familiar with the characters they were playing. In fact, they had played them for years. The relationships and subtext between them were already rich and well-established. I also hear stories of performance-capture shoots where actors are handed a large script, shoved into a mocap suit, and told to act. Cases like this tell me that the producers and directors have literally no experience in acting or drama. As a former actor, I still get insights into scenes I performed years ago. The material continues to cook inside of me. I wish all game cinematic producers and directors could grasp this understanding of how just a little more time and preparation can deepen and enrich a performance.

Discoveries or ideas tried out in rehearsal can bring the script to life but still need to be vetted in service of the story. Don't go off the rails with new ideas at rehearsal, as I once did. One of the characters was a very eccentric scientist, obsessive and grandiose. In a climactic sequence, while conducting experiments, she is cornered by the player and called out on her misuse of technology for genocidal purposes. She either must stop the experiment or be killed. I had the idea for her to laugh hysterically as she was being given the choice. Somewhere, I had seen hysterical laughter as an authentic but inappropriate response to danger. Unfortunately, when seeing the scene later in post, it didn't work at all. Because the character's movements were all based around laughter, we couldn't even change it with later dubbing. I still regret that I allowed what I thought was a cool idea to hijack the scene.

A good director can create freedom while maintaining discipline. A rehearsal day needs both. Use rehearsal as an exploration, and remember that shoot day, when the stakes are high, requires a different set of directing skills than rehearsal day. "On the movie set, it's a lot of freedom, a lot of planning and prep, everybody is free to speak their mind. At the same time, it's really efficient, it's not chaotic," film director Ron Shelton told NPR. "I believe it's like jazz…learn the chord changes before you improvise. In other words, the more we're prepared, as a crew, as a cast, as a production, the more we can breathe, and let loose, on the moment I say action. But if you're trying to play catch up, you can't get there. If you're trying to figure out what the chord changes are, you're never going to get there."

**BOX 8.1: The Meanings of Rehearsal**

The etymology of the word rehearsal points to its roots in French reheaser "to repeat…to turn the soil again." In the Renaissance, the word took on its present meaning of preparing for a dramatic presentation. In her book, *Respect for Acting*, the great actor and teacher Uta Hagen favors the German word for rehearsal, "die probe." Personally, I love the idea of rehearsal as a probe.

As of this writing, the technical demands and costs of performance-capture have a massive similarity to the practice of theater. Body movement data, vocal performance, and facial capture must be carefully synchronized, and any cuts within a scene become prohibitively expensive to stitch together. Therefore, scenes are addressed much in the same way as in a play: They must run in real time, from beginning to end, with no stops or pickups in the middle of the scene.

A group of actors in a performance-capture scene must be as honed and responsive as in a Broadway or West End theater company of top professionals. I don't know how a high level of performance can be reached without a day of rehearsal. Some productions rehearse in the morning and shoot in the afternoon, and some get performers into a mocap suit and shoot with no rehearsal at all. My own experience is that rehearsal, "the probe," is the only opportunity to dive beneath the superficial words, gestures and relationships in a busy and expensive production.

## The Performance Director's Cookbook

*Recipes for Table Read*

1. Actors, development team (dev team or devs), and writers meet, either physically or virtually. All receive printed or digital copies of a full script. Everyone introduces themselves and says the role they play in the production. (Remember, this is also about the first meeting of people who will be working closely with one another.)
2. Dev team gives a presentation on the core values and themes running through the game and shows artwork

and environments to give a visual feeling of what the final experience for the player will look and feel like. If the game is part of a series, previous iterations of the game are discussed.

3. Actors have full permission to perform or simply read. Someone reads stage directions and action descriptions. (For my own table reads, I ask actors who aren't in every scene to take turns reading the descriptions. They are usually delighted to do so.)
4. Between scenes, the Dev team narrates what sort of gameplay experiences the players are having. In-game lines to be recorded in VO are also read out loud. (Again, this is probably the only time the cinematic and gameplay dialogue will be read together. The in-game dialogue will be recorded later, in a sound booth.) The reading is recorded. Questions, issues, and ideas from the actors or director are addressed and discussed.

*In another approach, the table read is more like a rehearsal:*

1. Actors have received their scripts in advance.
2. Dev team gives their presentation.
3. Each scene is read and worked through, with director's notes and adjustments.
4. Actors give suggestions on story beats or dialogue changes. These suggestions are then tried out.
5. Blocking videos, previs animatics, or floor maps are reviewed. If the performances are primarily VO, improv or exploration between the actors is encouraged. They may never be in the same room at the same time again.

*Recipes for Workshop*

1. Everyone has received materials in advance and reviewed them. Workshop participants gather either in a room or virtually.
2. Broad scope notes are reviewed and dev team articulates their vision, supported by visuals.
3. Director or other creatives pitch their vision and ideas for scenes and a consensus is formed (or tabled for future discussion).

4. Scene by scene, the settings and environments, sets, and props are discussed. Stunts are sketched out. The idea is that everyone will be on the same page by the time the shoot begins.
5. Representatives from the mocap studio are present for all or part of the discussion, and their questions and concerns are answered.

*In an alternative approach, all the above occurs as part of a blocking rehearsal:*

1. At the top of each scene, the devs digitally display the environment and map or tape the relevant sections of the set on the floor. It's important to make sure actors aren't walking through walls or over cliffs.
2. The group—which may include only some actors, or often none at all—divides up the acting roles so there are enough bodies for blocking out the movement of the characters. ("Mitra, you play Sylvia and the colonel. Marcus will be the player. Can we get some animators to be the soldiers? Let's give them weapons.")
3. If actors have been brought in, they have received scripts in advance and may have learned the lines.
4. The atmosphere is one of experimentation and discovery. The scenes are video recorded or photographed for reference.

*Recipes for Rehearsal*

1. Short read through of scenes. Questions are discussed and answered.
2. Actors walk through blocking or create blocking on the spot. Beats that are not working are improvised or explored until they are solved.
3. Scenes are run for rough timing.

*In an extended first rehearsal, the procedure may be different:*

1. Body and vocal warmups set a tone of careful attention and presence.

2. Actors and director (and even writers) swap stories and share personal connections in a deep dive into the material. The atmosphere is open, safe, and collaborative.
3. Each actor does some off-script work—such as improvisation or reading with action choices—around the spine of their character. Adjustments are suggested to align the explorations with the story and tone of the game.
4. Key scenes are rehearsed or explored, even if they are not on the schedule for the upcoming shoot.
5. An ensemble feeling takes shape and becomes the basis for the rest of the capture sessions and recordings over the course of the production.

## References

*Battlefield 3.* Developed by DICE, Electronic Arts, 2011.

*Battlefield 4.* Developed by DICE, Electronic Arts, 2013.

Hagen, Uta, and Haskel Frankel. *Respect for Acting*. Macmillan Publishing Co., Inc., 1973.

*Killzone: Shadow Fall.* Developed by Guerrilla Games, Sony Computer Entertainment, 2013.

*Restrepo.* Directed by Tim Hetherington and Sebastian Junger, National Geographic Entertainment, 2010.

Shelton, Ron. "Just Getting Started." Interview by Elvis Mitchell, *The Treatment*, NPR, 20 Dec. 2017.

*Star Wars Jedi: Survivor.* Developed by Respawn Entertainment, Electronic Arts, 2023.

"Suzanne Shepherd." *Wikipedia*, Wikimedia Foundation, 7 Dec. 2024, en.wikipedia.org/wiki/Suzanne_Shepherd. Accessed 7 Dec. 2024.

*The Jungle Book.* Directed by Jon Favreau, performances by Neel Sethi, Bill Murray, and Idris Elba, Walt Disney Pictures, 2016.

Vallee, Jean-Marc. "Working with Strong Female Leads." *Sharp Objects*, HBO, 19 July 2018.

# 9
# Directing in the Volume

**In This Chapter**

- Respecting the actor's instrument
- The night before director's prep
- Leadership on set and in the booth
- Giving supportive adjustments
- Troubleshooting Q&A

Let's start this chapter with three scenes …

**Scene A**. I'm both acting and directing in this piece and I wonder if I've made a mistake by doing so. The other actor isn't giving me what I want, so I have to come up with something—and fast. So, I take my fellow actor for a ride. I put them in a large pan and push them around on the floor until we are both laughing as hard as we can. Then I stuff candies in my ears and dare the actor to try to get them out before I call "Cut!" The shot is perfect.

The actor is two years old.

The actor is my daughter.

**Scene B**. A character has to stop a terrorist attack, but I still don't feel a sense of urgency in this scene, which is primarily physical and has almost no dialogue. We try take after take until finally I ask him to jog beside me. We run around the room faster and faster saying the dialogue without stopping, until I jump out and call "Action!" and the actor runs into the scene.

This time, the urgency is there. It feels authentic.

Afterward I ask the actor what had stopped him from doing it that way earlier.

"I'm not sure," he says. "It just wasn't the way I saw it in my head."


DOI: 10.1201/9781003558910-10

**Scene C**. A young woman has taken her recently deceased father's car without permission and banged it up in a street race. The car now belongs to her older brother, who idolizes the memory of their father. The father's ride was his pride and joy, a hand-customized labor of love. The scene where she reveals the wreck to her brother should feel devastating but comes off as petulant and annoying.

There's literally no real emotion in the room, and I know I have to take a risk.

I gather the actors in a huddle and share a personal story about a devastating confrontation with my own brother, who we found in his apartment nearly dead, his body and brain ravaged by HIV. I described the scene in the apartment: half-eaten pizzas, doughnuts, and protein powders spilled everywhere. Vitamins and pills in piles on the table. Dirty clothes, bodily fluids, bills piled up, shuttered windows. It was a scene of shame, of hiding, of desperation. I describe the shock of seeing the shadow side of my high-flying, risk-taking, fun-loving brother.

I feel like maybe I've shared too much, but the energy in the room changes and the scene begins to take shape.

For the rest of the production, my actors and I share a rich, deep connection.

## CONNECTING WITH THE CAST

Part of my preparation as a director is taking care of the cast members and making sure they have what they need. I give actors as much preparation time as possible. I ask all the development teams I work with to send scripts—even if incomplete—to the actors at least two weeks ahead of production. This is especially important for performance capture, where lines must be memorized. I give actors my contact information in case they want to discuss the work. There is nothing I love more than when an actor takes me up on it. For one game, we had hour-long conference calls with each of the principal players before the first rehearsal. It was wonderful to talk about the themes and get the actors' ideas and questions on the table in advance. (Figure 9.1).

**Figure 9.1** Connecting with actors Dan Southworth, Jeff Branson, Kevin Dorman, and Leith Burke on a performance capture set from *Killzone Shadow Fall.* (Courtesy of Guerrilla Games. Photo by Katja Kulenkampff.)

### What's the Scene About?

You've read all the scripts and done your homework. You know the themes of the piece, and you know what they mean to you. You have looked at each character and identified their spine, what means most to them at this point in their life. You've looked at each scene and you know how it fits into the overall arc of the game. You have a rough idea of the blocking and what the environment looks like. You know what just happened for each character in the scenes, and you have candidates for both the surface action and the subtextual action for each character. You have ideas for where the beats of each scene begin and end, and you have candidates for the climax or turning point of the scene. You can sum everything up and say, with confidence, "This scene is about X."

You've done all the preparation and now comes the day. You're terrified! Will they get it? Will the actors be good? What if they hate me? What if my ideas don't work? What if, what if, what if … At the base of these insecurities is a flawed premise: *I, the director, am responsible for what we get. I alone am responsible for what the actors do. And if they don't do it well, it's my fault.*

This is an unwinnable perspective. Remember, there are no emergencies in animation. It's not brain surgery. I once asked an anesthesiologist how he handled the pressure of being responsible for someone's life or death during surgery. His reply surprised me. "I don't see myself as solely being able to control whether someone lives or dies. I'm part of a system, a medical team that functions as a unit. I'm a cog in a wheel." It's like being a performance director. You need good material, good actors, good technology, and a willing and responsive team to make the magic.

Directing in the booth or the volume is like directing at a rehearsal, workshop, or audition. In fact, I always encourage directors to be present to direct the candidates at call-back auditions. I learn so much from directing auditions. I get a feeling for which actors resonate with my ideas as I begin to unpack the scenes. The lack of pressure to deliver is freeing. I can't imagine having to deliver performance-level scenes without having tried the material out somewhere.

This is easier if you are directing pcap than voice-over. Sometimes when I work on a game that is only voice-over, I'll organize a table read or even arrange my own solo read in my office—a cast of one for an audience of one—just to see what strikes me. By reading out loud, by walking the set alone, by moving dolls, a director gets out of their head and into their body. Just as an actor must. And when the director and actor get out of their heads and into their bodies, the scenes reveal themselves. So, on the day of, a director needs to prepare to be in their body, too.

### Caring for the Actor: The Body as the Instrument

No matter how little or how extensively a director has prepared, that preparation takes a back seat the moment they get in front of an actor. As a director, your physical presence, your face, your voice, your gestures all have a profound effect on the actor. Studies of choir leaders show their gestures and physical positioning and even their faces can change the sound quality of the singers. The actors will be keenly attuned to your response to their work. You are not treating them like puppets. You are treating them as master artists, trusting their brilliance and natural impulses to bring the scene alive. When it isn't as alive as it can be or isn't attaining the vision you have for the scene, you cleverly adjust the imaginary circumstances to steer the scene in a different direction. You aren't there to bully, harangue, or demand that anyone comply. You are there to be a support, a guide, and a coach, to keep the actors focused on the circumstances and the emotional stakes of the scene. Whether you share a story, change an action, suggest an "as if" or give a technical voice or movement note, the key is to demonstrate that you support and believe in your actors. If the actor feels you're in their corner, they will, more often than not, give you back 150%.

A large part of caring for the actor, particularly in the demanding physical and vocal realm of videogames, is a healthy respect for the actor's body as their instrument. A sore toe, a strained knee, or a torn shoulder can sideline an actor from working. A swollen vocal cord or strained tissue in a voice actor's throat can not only delay production, but also harm the actor's voice and keep them from earning their living. Almost every actor who has worked on a videogame has a horror story of pulling a muscle or losing their voice, spurred on by demanding directors with no respect for an actor's limits. An actor is not a floor-polishing machine. Don't run them until the tank is empty and you damage the engine.

### BOX 9.1: PCAP Directing Prep: The Seven Night-Before Questions

Tomorrow's the day you are going on the directing floor in front of your audience of actors, developers and technicians. Don't panic! Here are seven questions to help you ground yourself in the work you've already done. This is not a new assignment for the night before; think of it as a review. If you even focus on one of these questions, you will have plenty to work with.

1. **What are the Themes Presented in the Piece?** Remind yourself of the themes you've been playing with and your personal relationship to them. Revisit your vision of the piece and how you want it to go. Are there any obstacles to that? Think back or review notes about themes that are important to the developers. Gather the research

you've done and decide whether you need any additional information.

2. **What is the Spine for Each Character, Based on the Facts and the Situation?** This usually begins in casting. Is what you identified earlier still relevant, or is there a stronger choice? Have alternates in mind as well.
3. **What More Can You Learn about the Material to Be Shot?** Read over the scenes for the day. For each scene, boil down your ideas into one main action for each character. One way Judith Weston phrases it is, "Why did this character come here today? What would be their ideal outcome at the end of the scene?" Have something for each character, no matter how small the role.
4. **Can You Identify the PTA of Your Scenes from Memory?** Remember, P (place), T (time), A (action). If you can't think of anything else, as long as you know these, you'll have a solid foundation for the basics of the scene.
5. **What More Can I Learn about the *Event* of the Scene?** Have a few options for the moment when the power dynamic changes. Who gets what they want and who doesn't? Break each scene into beats and have an action for each character as steps toward their goal. A good metaphor for this is the way sailors "tack," zig-zagging toward their destination depending on the direction of the wind.
6. **Where Are We Now?** Revisit the rehearsal or shoot days already completed. See if you still feel the same way about the scenes or characters from your original prep. Are scenes already shot showing you that the character is developing in another direction?
7. **Are There Visuals I Need as Inspiration or for Staging?** Gather any blocking or previs videos or floor maps. Make sure they are properly labeled and you have easy access to them. You don't want the whole crew standing around while you hunt for your materials.

## Directing Days

Make sure you begin your day properly, with time to center and focus. Don't over-schedule or create a scenario where you barely have time to get to the set or studio. Of course, many of us who are performance directors find that challenging. We have kids to feed and drop off at school, pets to walk, and doctor appointments to be squeezed in. We're also finding the next gig while working on the one we have.

This is where the lifestyle you have created for yourself either bears fruit or robs you of energy. A director—or any creative artist, for that matter—provides most of their value through their creativity. So: Are you prioritizing it? Are you keeping the pump primed by surrounding yourself with stimulating and nurturing people, developing healthy lifestyle habits, exercising, and getting plenty of rest? This is especially challenging for working parents. I was one myself while my daughter was growing up. By periodically taking classes in acting or directing, having good books by my bedside, and maintaining a lifelong meditation practice, I developed the ability to make micro-shifts in my state of mind. Simply sitting in the car or in a quiet corner of the studio, standing outside and taking a deep breath, or sending a quick text or making a call to a loved one is often enough to shift me back to my creative center. And if you've done your directing homework, both inspiration and the fruits of your preparation will be there when you need them.

### *Arriving to the Volume*

The performance capture volume is a busy place at the beginning of the day. The actors have come earlier than the director to get into their mocap suits and to have their body and face markers applied. They do their **ROMS**—a series of bodily and facial movements to calibrate the cameras so the technicians can keep track of all those dots. (Figures 9.2 and 9.3).

**Figure 9.2** Performance capture actor Anna Vargha being led through a range of motion sequence to calibrate the cameras.

**Figure 9.3** An example of ROMs (range of motion) movements.

Get there in time to set up your equipment—your "station." On the pcap stage, I have my own chair, a bottle of water, my computer, a copy of the day's schedule, and the latest version of the script.

Greet the cast and crew. If you have any questions, this is the time to ask them. Simply saying "Good morning ... how are you feeling today?" shows the cast that you are here for them and gives them an opening to share what's on their mind. The starting point for the day is knowing the emotional temperature of the people you are working with. After the cast and crew assemble for a safety meeting and announcements, I usually lead the actors in a warmup. By gathering your cast for a last-minute pep-talk, you are setting the tone as a leader.

### BOX 9.2: Leader as Collaborator

Always remember that as a performance director, you are serving the needs of the development team. I once had a very insightful dream where my awareness was located in the body of a game developer. We were about to go into the studio to record dialogue for our project—a project that we had worked on for years, a project that was our baby. I had some anxiety that I was handing my "child" over to a voice director who didn't have the same level of ownership as my team.

I awoke with the startling revelation that I had been approaching the work all wrong. I was often at loggerheads with my creative teams, who I felt were too mired in their preexisting notions about the direction of the scenes. I now understood that even if I needed to free the developers from their preconceptions, it was my obligation as a performance director to honor their ownership of the game as well. I saw that, as a visiting collaborator, I would never be successful in trying to break the bond between the "parents" (the developers) and the "child" (the game). Instead, I needed to find out as much as possible about the team's expectations and ideas, and filter my own unique perspective through theirs. I consider this dream one of the greatest gifts from my unconscious, and will never forget it.

*Speaking to the Actors*

Each day you direct actors, come with a fresh basket of ideas. You will only use them if you need to. Always let the actor do it their way first; pay attention to what they naturally bring to the role. Ask questions, and let the actors ask questions. Above all, listen.

In the volume, review a rehearsal or blocking video and let the actors do what I call a "stumble through." Let them take a stab at the scene with the freedom to make mistakes and ask questions. Modify any blocking that isn't working and then do a rehearsal take at 75% effort. Give notes on specific beats or pacing. Pick it up here, pause a little there. Use actor-speak as much as possible. "Pause and let his words sink in." Or, "Keep the pace up. As if your taxi is waiting outside with the meter running. Every extra second costs you."

The obvious direction might seem to be, "a little faster, please." But that could cause the actor to mechanically speed up and lose the subtlety of the scene. Always try to think of something imaginative. "This time, you want to make sure you get as many answers as you can before the authorities get here." Or to slow it down, you might suggest, "Ask these questions carefully so you don't upset him." Use phrases like *maybe* or *what if.* These qualifiers position your notes as ideas for a collaborator instead of commands to a subordinate. "What if she really does like him, and is setting him up to forgive her when she pistol-whips him and escapes with their boat?" The actor can then say, "I like that idea," or they are free to say something like, "No, I want him to think I like him. Then when I take the boat, I'll crush all his hopes."

When giving an adjustment, *never give* ***result-oriented direction.*** Result-oriented direction means saying something like, "Be angrier." That's just another version of giving a line reading, which is another big no-no that marks you as unprepared or as a rank amateur. Instead, speak in the language of acting and shift the circumstances: "She's the woman who killed your brother." Draw on your preparation and any discussions or things you've learned about the actor. If they mentioned something about childcare when they came in, use it later to create imaginary scenarios: "He threatened your kid on the grounds of the school." You can skillfully weave together the world of the game with what you know about the actor's life and experience.

Taking an actor aside privately is another excellent and effective way to give adjustments in a manner that respects the actor without shaming them in front of the rest of the cast and crew. It's also imaginative and fun to give your actors a "secret" adjustment that keeps their scene partner guessing. Whisper in their ear something like, "This time, try a charm offensive. Make them feel like a million bucks." And maybe to the other person in the scene, "Take in what they say, but stay on the alert in case they try to bully you into something." Adjustments like these keep the actors on their toes. They will watch each other's reactions very carefully to see if they're meeting their objective. *Remember, the best kind of actions or objectives are the ones where a character wants to have an effect on another character.*

Actors—especially high-profile ones—can bristle at receiving notes. I've had actors patronizingly smile and nod and then ignore what I suggest. I've even had one actor roll their eyes at a suggestion and say, "Really?" If this happens, take it in and back off briefly, but never abandon the actor. Often they are testing you to see how committed you are to your vision. Stick to the facts of the scene until you gain the actor's trust. The PTAs contain all the information an actor really needs to know anyway. No matter how famous an actor is, your job is to help them do *their* job. And if they are doing their job well, get the hell out of the way.

## The Performance' Director's FAQ

### *What If They're Not Getting It?*

Asking this question usually means that you're giving result-oriented direction. You may be too stuck on a pre-planned idea of what "getting it" means. Maybe the actor has discovered something fresh about the scene or the character that could be interesting. Are you clear about the character's action? Have you given the actor a juicy subtext? Only on the rarest occasion is an actor so miscast that they must be replaced. In that case, finish out the day and have a frank discussion with the team and the actor's agent. But first, make sure your direction is clear and specific.

If an actor is getting overstimulated from too much direction, back off. Reassure your actor that you are behind them, and help them get back to trusting their instincts.

*How Do I Get an Actor Out of Their Comfort Zone?*

The way to get an actor out of their comfort zone is to make them feel comfortable with the discomfort of exploration. Create a welcoming atmosphere for risk. If an actor is playing it safe and not going deep enough, first see what you, as the director, might need to change. Have you created a deep rapport with your actor? Have you created a safe space for them to try things and fail? Are you being too rigid about your expectations? Have you shared how the story/scene/moment parallels something in your own life? Take the risk of sharing something personal with them. Take your actor aside or have a meal with them. Praise their efforts and ask how you can support them in going further. Be supportive but honest. The last thing you want them to feel is that they are failing. Try letting them improvise the scene and do it wrong, or in their own way. Free up the material.

*What If an Actor Is Having Mental Health Issues?*

Actors are very sensitive creatures, and their insecurities and issues may come up during the work day. Give them space to have their feelings or take a break if they need to. Reassure the actor that they belong and they are safe to bring their whole self to the material. Check in with them after a particularly emotionally taxing scene. Do they need a break to recover? It's also a very good idea to check in with the actors at the end of the day. Thank them for their work—and make sure they feel complete with what they did today.

*What If You Think Substance Abuse May Be Hampering the Actor?*

If substances are involved, handle it extremely delicately. Discuss their performance with the team and have someone make a careful call to the actor's team. Reaffirm how important the actor is to the project. Ask the agent if the actor has had any issues with substances. Communicate the expectations that the actor be sober, prepared, and ready to work.

*How Do I Deal with Conflicts between Cast Members? If an Actor Doesn't Feel Safe with Another Actor?*

When conflicts arise between cast members, make sure there are good boundaries in place regarding the work. What is the source of the conflict? Is one actor giving inappropriate feedback to another? Make sure everyone knows that only the director gives adjustments to actors. Have you, as a director, set an open and collaborative tone at the beginning of the production? Have you also set up boundaries at the beginning? Talk to each actor separately if it seems appropriate and only if the work is being affected. Stay out of the personal dramas from behind the scenes if you can. If there is inappropriate behavior going on, address it professionally through appropriate channels, such as HR. If there are issues with intimate scenes, make sure you have hired an intimacy coordinator so that everyone feels safe.

*What Do I Do When It Seems I Need to Be More Strict with Actors?*

There is a fine line between a friendly, collaborative set and an overly permissive one. What is "too loose?" Are actors not arriving prepared? Are they late for their call or wandering off and causing delays? The morning meeting is a good place to address these issues without calling anyone out personally. Especially when you have days with a large cast, reaffirm that you would like everyone's cooperation in paying attention and staying on set so they are ready when called. Encourage actors to work on their own when they are not in the scenes, to get together with scene partners and run lines. Keep them involved even when they are not working.

*What Do I Do When a Big Life Event Is Affecting an Actor's—Or the Whole Cast's—Performance? Or Even Their Ability to Come to the Set?*

The first and most important thing is to acknowledge what is happening and how it might affect the cast and crew. Years ago, when I was in drama school, we were taught that a professional should "leave their problems at the stage door." But some problems are too big to leave: the death of a loved one, a disaster of any kind, a diagnosis of an illness. The most important thing to do is to acknowledge what is happening. If it's a personal event, express your support to the actor and try to make accommodations for their schedule as much as possible. A VO session can always be rescheduled, and the great thing about mocap is that another actor can stand in and the voice and face replaced later. I just was involved in a shoot where a lead actor tested positive for COVID-19 the day before the shoot. While it made scheduling difficult, a stunt actor stepped in and the affected actor was able to provide a temporary voice virtually. Larger civil and cultural disasters can be acknowledged at the morning meeting. As much as is authentically possible, a director needs to rise to the position of a compassionate leader. A good director is able to help the actor channel any feelings into the work. I received a message from an actor who was very good but kept stumbling over their lines during the shoot. Months later, the actor told me that the night before the shoot she had separated from her spouse. "I wasn't my best, but you were kind and gracious and grounded me just with your presence." A director's supportive presence is their number one job on the set.

*What Do I Do When I Feel That a Line or Scene Is Inappropriate and Do Not Want to Ask an Actor to Perform It?*

Appropriateness is a very subjective evaluation. What about the moment seems inappropriate? Does the scene go against a value held personally by the actor? Is it out of tune for the character, or gratuitous in some way? Have you previously flagged the scene to the writers or development team? What do the actors say about it? The few times this has come up in my career, we were able to handle it advance. It was either not problematic for the actors (only for me), or was flagged by higher ups and eventually cut. Occasionally we've had to pause and discuss alternatives, which often means doing a take as written and then doing an alternative.

*What Do I Do When an Actor Refuses to Say a Line or Perform a Scene?*

This situation has arisen from time to time. What is the reason the actor is refusing? Is there a moral reason or is it a question of taste? Listen carefully to the actor's reasoning and take it seriously. If you have already set the tone for a collaborative set, bring the actor's concerns, or the actor themselves, to a meeting with the development team and the writers. As a director, you have the authority to demand that the actor comply. But such a demand may have repercussions that may poison your collaborative relationship with the actor. This is where a director's skills at negotiation come into play. Where there is consensus, there is happiness. Listen deeper to what the actor's motivation might be. Sometimes, there are other issues driving this refusal: They may be unhappy with the direction of the character, or with how many shooting days they're being given, or with their pay. If the actor is a celebrity, they may be looking for a "win" to show their power. It can feel like the hardest thing in the world to stand your ground with a celebrity. You may not win in the end, but don't think of it as winning or losing. Make sure you have the consensus of the team who are your employers, and make the best choice you can at the moment. Make requests to the actor and get their agreement that you will provide them with scripts in advance and that they will need to inform you about any objections before the shoot day. Make sure to avoid having to make decisions under time pressure.

*What If the Development Team Disagrees with My Choices or Direction?*

If you have done your homework and verbalized your choices in advance with the development team, it's always possible to defend your position with the facts of the scene. The main strategy here is to always listen and be open to their input. Consider your development team as collaborators and avoid being dictatorial. Remember, it takes many people to make a game and they all have a stake in the outcome. A performance director for a game is not like a filmmaker with a singular perspective in telling a story. Rather, you are a skilled specialist tasked with helping the team realize their vision through the actors' performances.

*What If Someone Else Gives an Actor Adjustments?*

Unfortunately, this happens frequently on game sets. There are so many sub-teams with stakeholders that may circulate in and out depending on the level of the game being worked on. Set the tone early on by explaining to your collaborators the reasons for channeling all feedback through you. When other people give the actor direction, there may be conflicts with what the performance director has told them. There's nothing worse than confusion on the set as to who is in charge. If a department has particularly complex feedback—for instance, regarding the movements an actor must make for the sake of game play—I will often ask the appropriate person to explain to both me and the actor at the same time. That way I know what is being asked for and discussed and can help translate the direction into actor language. At the same time, it reinforces the boundary that all feedback to actors goes through the director.

## References

Grady, Melissa LeAnn *The Effects of Nonverbal Behaviors Exhibited by Multiple Conductors on the Timbre, Intonation, and Perceptions of Three University Choirs, and Assessed Relationships Between Time Spent in Selected Conductor Behaviors and Analyses of the Choirs' Performances.* Doctoral Dissertation, University of Kansas, 2014. Retrieved from https://hdl.handle.net/1808/15512.

Shewell, Christina. *Voice Work: Art and Science in Changing Voices.* Wiley-Blackwell, 2010.

*Star Wars Battlefront 2.* Developed by Electronic Arts, DICE, Motive Studios, and Criterion Games, Electronic Arts, 2017.

Steinhauer, Kimberly, Mary McDonald Klimek, and Jo Estill. *The Estill Voice Model: Theory & Translation.* Estill Voice International, LLC, 2017.

# 10
# Directing in the Voiceover Booth

**In This Chapter**

- The roles in a voice recording session
- The importance of voice training
- VO pre-production and scripts
- Running the recording session
- Efforts and barks
- Caring for the voice

As a talent coordinator, I'm sitting in on a voiceover session with a producer/director and an actor. The scene is a classic interactive situation: the player approaches a character, and after hitting a trigger point, the character addresses the player with some important bit of information or story theme. The producer gives the voice artist the following direction:

"It's that moment when you are waiting around by a big vase. You know that sound? Waiting around by a big vase? It really should sound like, you know, waiting around by a big vase."

I'm dying inside at this crude, nonsensical direction, but as I am only a coordinator, low in the pecking order, I can't say anything.

Eager to please and possibly get called in again for another job, the actor replies, "Oh! OK, yes, I definitely know that sound."

And then they read the line again, a little bit louder.

Is this good language to use to direct an actor? My hope is that you have read my first few chapters and you know that "to wait around" is a dull, non-playable action. You understand that, instead, the actor needs Place, Time, and Action. You'll be able to use that image of waiting around by a big vase as a Place, and you'll add Time and Action: "You


DOI: 10.1201/9781003558910-11

are concealing yourself behind a large stone vase after the attacks on your village. It's a good place to have a covert conversation with the player, to find out if they can help you locate your missing loved ones."

Voice acting in a game is delivered many ways, through cinematics, approaches, **branching dialogue**, **in-game** shouts and efforts, **idles**, alternate endings, open environments, and through **player-chosen** characters. With all these different forms of dialogue, voice directing a game in the sound booth is a wonderful creative challenge requiring superb concentration, deep listening, total flexibility, and excellent organization (Figure 10.1).

**Figure 10.1** The author directing voice actor Dave Fennoy in a recording studio.

### Responsibilities in a Voice Recording Session

Everyone in a recording session has a job to do. In the best professional sessions, each team member is focused on their role and attends 100% to that role while supporting others in their roles. When the roles aren't clearly defined and start to overlap, things get messy, and the acting suffers. Along with clear roles and responsibilities, there must be collaboration. A good voice director is an individual who can balance the needs of the game and sound teams with the needs of the actor.

*Voice Director*

The voice director runs the recording session and coaches the acting, in consultation with the development team and the engineer. There may also be a note-taker in the session. As with performance capture, only the voice director should give the actor notes and adjustments. Remote recording—when the director and the team are not physically present with the actor in the booth—makes this harder. I often feel like I'm on a game show where I have to hit the button to speak before a boundary-challenged developer rushes in to tell the actor how to do it better. It takes a gentle but firm approach to keep the lines of communication clear.

The voice director is also responsible for the pacing of the session while carefully monitoring the actor's energy level and vocal quality. A high rate of **LPH**—lines per hour—may be the criteria for getting hired, or a point of pride for the director, but if the actor's voice is tiring and becoming ragged, raspy, or "thick," it's imperative that recuperative breaks be given to the actor. Taking care of the actor, and the actor's instrument—their voice and body—comes out of a deep respect for the actor and the amount of effort it takes to perform their material.

*Recording Engineer*

Recording engineers have a complex set of tasks all their own. They set up all the equipment, adjust the microphones for the talent, balance the recording levels, start and stop the recording process, and often mark **selects**—the takes the director wants to keep to go directly into the game—as they go. Recording engineers are highly trained listeners who monitor every nuance, crackle, and change in sound. They are the only other person who should talk directly to the actor, asking them to repeat a phrase or change the position of their mouth in relation to the mic. The recording engineer will hand off the recorded material to the editors and is ultimately responsible for the quality of the recording.

*Note-Taker/Assistant*

The engineer is usually assisted by a note-taker, who marks down the numbers of the **takes** and **reads**, which of the reads is the selected take, and notes what the **alternate** takes might hold. With the massive production pipeline of recorded voice material in a game, sometimes in the tens of thousands of lines, this is a very important role. In a few months or a year, when a line isn't working with the material because something has changed and a sound designer needs to find an alternate line, these notes will be a lifeline for the team.

*Producer*

The producer role can be filled by anyone on the development team who has in-depth knowledge of the game and how the voice acting will be used. It can be a producer or assistant producer, a writer, a creative director, or a sound designer. They are ultimately responsible for getting the team's needs met in the recording sessions, and the best way for them to do that is to support the voice director by being able to answer questions, to supply the PTA if it's not in the script, and to be able to make a judgment call on creative decisions, such as character choices or line changes. The producer can also weigh in on practical decisions such as which material is the priority for the day or whether to let an actor go home early if their voice is getting fatigued. The producer should never attempt to compete with the voice director for the actor's attention or for the right to direct the actor. I've had both of these happen, and guess what? Something always goes wrong. An actor gets confused or upset, lines get missed, or the PTA is incorrect. It's important that producers understand what their job is and what it isn't. Instead of getting involved in the actor/director relationship, the producer should communicate clearly with the director to let them know whether what they are getting from the actor fits into the larger context of the game. They should make sure any notes from the production team are conveyed to the director and are up to date. Producers need to stay focused on the session, supporting the voice director.

**Collaboration**

I personally am never comfortable directing a VO session on a game without a member of the development team present. As a contractor, I simply don't know enough about the game's details to get the right sound. Yet, I've heard stories about voice directors who don't allow the game team to be present, argue with the team about choices or never supply alternate reads. Many voice directors don't even review the script before the session. When a director I know told me they don't look at the material before the session, I was astonished. "Why don't you?" I asked. They answered, "I just like to be in the moment." While I can appreciate being in the moment, the director still needs to serve the game and the story. Knowing the PTA goes a long way toward guiding the actor into acting truthfully within the circumstances of the game.

The voice director's job is not to be a dictator or puppet master. Instead, see yourself as a specialist who speaks actor language and understands how videogames are made. You are using your special knowledge and sensitivity to actors to help your game developers get quality acting into their game. You are a leader for this part of the process, and you set the tone of a collaborative environment for the team. You also teach the team how to organize their materials, how to develop their audition pieces and how to format their scripts. If consistently serving the needs of others as part of a creative team makes you feel worn down and like a victim, this is not the job for you. You have to serve the team. You will be able to make a huge creative contribution to the team. Feel good about it, but don't get a swelled head and think you know all. I was asked by a voice producer at a large company, who hires many voice directors, to give you this message: "Just Don't be an asshole."

Stay flexible. The team has more invested in this baby than you do.

### Voice Training

Ideally, anyone hoping to perform or direct VO will have training and experience in voice, movement, and acting. While this may seem like an impossibly high bar to entry, why not aim for it? There are many fine voice directors who come in from writing or game design or even sound engineering, but they should still aim for a high degree of craft and excellence. How does someone without proper training make up the difference? An acting class with a great teacher is an excellent place to start or return to for any actor, director, or writer. For anyone coaching actors in voice, Estill Voice Training, which teaches through an anatomically based approach, the Linklater Voice Method, and the Rodenburg Technique, are among many good sources of practice.

Anyone directing with minimal technical knowledge of the voice should, at the very least, have a good support system of advisors. One of my own teachers, Patsy Rodenburg, who was a voice coach for the Royal Shakespeare Company for 40 years, gave me invaluable advice when I was directing my first audiobook. I was remarking how my author had a habit of starting out strong and then dropping down in tone. Pasty simply asked me about the "geography," and I realized that so much of the author's sound issues had to do with the placement of the text in relation to her posture and position. It was a simple fix for the marathon reading sessions of an audiobook and gave consistency to her voice and breath control.

The human voice is a miraculous expression of body, mind, and soul. On a basic physical level, without the breath and the parts of the body that act as resonators, a human voice would sound like a bee in a handkerchief. The vocal folds, two small pieces of tissue about the size of the nail on your little finger, sit in the larynx and change size and shape, open and close, and respond instantaneously to the intention to convey sound. The jaw, the lips, the teeth, tongue, throat, nose, and soft palate all come into play when shaping sound. The resonating chambers of the nasopharynx, the throat, the chest, the lungs, the diaphragm, and the whole torso power the voice with the breath. We then shape that sound into language with the articulators of the mouth. Once we've learned how to use our voices as toddlers, most people never again think consciously about how to use our voice. It just happens.

From the time I was nine years old until I graduated from high school at age 17, I was plagued by problems with my teeth. I had numerous rounds of braces, rubber bands, retainers, and surgeries to correct some abnormalities in my mouth and jaw. When I arrived as a young actor at drama school, I was shocked to discover I had developed a lisp, a slushy "S" sound that was causing too much air to be released. The problem stemmed from a habit I had developed of sending the thin stream of air out the side of my mouth instead of straight ahead.

Fortunately, my drama school had a training program for speech therapists and I was assigned to work with one to correct my "s." I'm extremely grateful to have had this support, but the experience was excruciating. The movement of the tongue is normally an unconscious act. To suddenly have to think about retraining where I put the tip of my tongue took enormous effort. Just as the speech therapist was critical to my development, voice directors who know how voice and speech work are extremely helpful to actors. When you give an actor a quick technical adjustment that leads to a better sound or eases any strain, you earn the actor's trust and respect. They feel free to give even more because they know you are looking out for their instrument.

So much of voice training, whether for singing, acting, giving speeches, or debating, comes from imaginative prompts that sound "right." Unfortunately, what sounds right is often what is similar to the habitual patterns of the listener. When I first trained, years ago, everyone in the US, without fail, was taught to have a "general American" sound. The truth is, there is no such thing. America has as many accents as it has states and towns and cities. What is "general American" has changed over the years, but when I was studying, no one could have an accent that had any regional quality at all. Many actors forced themselves to never again speak in the accent of where they grew up.

Fortunately, all that has changed. Dudley Knight, of the University of California, Irvine, caused a sensation when he proposed that acting students retain their original patterns of speech. Instead, he offered the idea that actors learn how to make all the sounds of human speech, including the clicks and pops of Xhosa and Zulu, so they would be able to amend their speech patterns to fit the character. Accent work is critically important to anyone wishing to work as a voice actor. There is also much more emphasis on authenticity in accents today and there has been a push for casting actors who authentically grew up with the accent. But for any actor doing multiple voices and characters, the accents they use should be technically accurate. The University of Kansas has a wonderful free resource online with their IDEA catalogue, the International Dialects of English Archives. They have interviews with English speakers of different ages from all over the English-speaking world, as well as with English speakers who learned English as a second language.

### Pre-production for VO

For every voice directing job, I now insist on having a creative meeting with the team. Some teams feel they don't have time for such a meeting, and some sound studios—who are often acting as a contractor—are nervous about allowing direct contact between the voice director and the development team for fear that the director will steal the client away. This is detrimental, fear-based thinking. Nothing should get in the way of collaborators exchanging ideas.

As with pcap, VO scripts should be sent to actors in advance. The one caveat here is that voice scripts are usually in spreadsheet form, and they are not particularly easy for actors to make heads or tails of. Experienced voice actors will know what to look for. Less tech-savvy actors may not even be able to open it. If I'm in contact with the person on the team sending the scripts out, I might ask to include my email or phone number in case the actor has questions. Prepare early (make sure the developers prepare early, too) and get the actors the materials they need: The extra work is well worth it. If this initial acquaintance between actor and script isn't done in advance, it will have to be done at the session, which takes up costly recording time. Actors like to do homework too, and appreciate the chance to lay eyes on the material, even if briefly. It starts their unconscious processes and gives them a framework of questions to ask and potential connections to their own truth and lived experience.

Every voice directing job is different but remember that you are being hired to be a specialist, an actor-whisperer, to be the go-between. Always be ready to lead and educate your developers in preparing for a recording. There is nothing more wasteful, confusing, and chaotic than rockin' up to the director's chair, with an actor in the booth, and finding out the script is a mess, the actor has no idea what the game is about, and the team hasn't even met with you to talk about the project.

### Scripts

As we have discussed elsewhere, the script will likely be in a spreadsheet form. If you don't understand which column contains the text to be recorded, it's important to ask in advance. I once worked on a game where the spreadsheet was so confusing, not even the developer knew which column was to be recorded. We agreed on a particular column, spent several days recording it, only to find out later that was the wrong column.

Spreadsheets with thousands of lines usually have columns with a line number, a filename, a character name, the actual line to be recorded, and numerous other columns that are important to the developer but may or may not help the actor. Hopefully, there is a column with some PTA information, context or notes. There is often a column with other information such as intensity level, proximity to other characters, or type of line—for instance, a battle shout or a stealthy whisper.

One of the biggest drawbacks in working with spreadsheets is that the spreadsheet is sorted by character, so that all the lines for the same actor appear on one sheet. The problem then becomes that any line that is in response to another character's line will disappear. How is a director or actor to know what is a standalone statement and what is a reply? There is a range of potential answers to this maddening quandary. Try to get access to a master script that groups lines in conversations together. Ask if there is a secondary document that describes the gameplay and the lines that go along with particular actions. Unfortunately, these secondary solutions take up valuable time as you search for the corresponding information.

The best solution is to encourage your developers to make actor-friendly spreadsheets. Ask them to put the PTA in a special column. Insist they take the time to include other characters' responses to conversations. Your developers will be stressed out and overworked; they may complain that you are asking too much, but they know that these suggestions will absolutely make a better product and better VO for the game. If they can go even farther, you will ideally be able to play the other character's previously recorded line in a conversation for your actor to respond to. Even better, but extremely rare because of the cost and complexity, you will have actors recording together as an ensemble in a large booth.

The bottom line here is that the voice director needs to be prepared. Look at the script, listen to the references, and view any artwork for the character or the environment before you get into the session. This way, you will be able to ask the right questions, you will flag any potential problems before the session, and best of all, your actor will see by your actions that you are on their side and looking out for them.

### Running the Session

In the voiceover booth, as compared to the pcap volume, the director is less likely to have had advanced contact with the actor. Begin with greeting them and getting a sense of how their day is going. Find out if they know what they are working on, and if they have received or taken a look at the script. Let them know about any technical details such as how many characters they'll be doing, whether any of the recording is to picture—in other words, will there be a video reference to which the voiceover artist will perform—and most importantly, whether there might be vocal stress involved.

Be prepared to give a quick summary of the themes, the setting, and the details of Place, Time, and Action. Ask actors what *their* ideas are for the character. If the development team has expressed anything about what they are looking for, translate that for the actor into "actor language."

Make sure the actor has water and anything else they need to support their work. What is the geography—the positioning of the text relative to the actor's body? It's normally better if the actor stands, but actors come in all shapes, sizes, and abilities, so sitting may be a better option. Is the script font large enough and is there enough light to see the words? If the script is onscreen, can the actor see it? Is the mic in the way? Make sure the actors are set up to do their best work. They will feel and appreciate your care and support.

#### *Finding and Sustaining the Character*

If the character is new and hasn't been established, show the actor any artwork if you have access to it. A visual reference can really drive an actor's choices in an interesting and creative way. Describe any PTA or spine relating to this character as well. Keep it short and to the point.

Always let the actor do a read first; pay attention to what they naturally bring to the role. In the booth, let them read down the page and listen to where their voice is sitting on this particular day. Is the pitch and texture of their voice naturally fitting the character, or do they need to play around with an adjustment. If the actor has done the role previously, play any voice references to help them get into character and match the tone they used before. Voices can vary dramatically from day to day. A "listen and repeat" can be very helpful here. You play a line from one of their previous sessions and the actor repeats the line in the same way. (This is similar to a concertmaster playing a tone before the orchestra starts tuning.)

Start the recording with a single line and let the actor do three reads of the same line in a row, generally referred to as "a-b-c," with each letter standing in for a separate read. Give the actor some feedback, and move to the next line or do another take. Get consensus with your team and mark the selected take. As you move through the session and the actor gets more comfortable in the role, pick up speed if you need to accomplish a certain number of lines per hour. I usually start out slowly with my voice actors and create a rapport.

"Let's try a take. Three reads in a row, a-b-c, and feel free to make each a little different." The actor reads. "Very nice. I like the simplicity of the second read. Can you give me three more like that?" Actor reads again. "Great. Let's take read C if the team is good with that?" Then, I get consensus with the team. "Ok let's move on. This next line is a warning. Let the other characters know they better not mess with you." And so on.

If the actor's performance grows more confident as they go, make a mental note of where you are in the script. If you have time at the end of the session, go back to the lines the actor recorded at the start and re-record them. When you make this a regular practice, you'll feel more comfortable letting the actor explore the character in the early part of the session.

As voice director, adhere to the same artistic discipline we have discussed in earlier chapters. When the pressure is on, you'll feel tempted to give line reads and result-oriented direction. Train yourself to shift circumstances, suggest playable actions, give "as ifs," and use obstacles, images, personal stories, and all the other tools to prompt the actor and give them something to respond to.

Pace the actor's voice, especially with vocally stressful efforts and barks. Save those for the end of the session. (Never plan a full four-hour session of vocally stressful work. You will rarely, if ever, have good results after the first two hours.) Even though the director is generally the only one to give feedback to the actor, I sometimes keep the mic open to keep the actor in the loop with the team. Working this way keeps everyone in a team relationship.

**Efforts and Barks**

Perhaps the most misunderstood, dreaded, and often painful group of utterings in a game are the efforts and barks. But they don't have to be! Games are kinetic and normally involve walking, running, climbing, throwing, jumping, scaling, and moving heavy objects, in addition to shooting, stabbing, choking, drowning, falling, and myriad other ways to die and be reborn. Characters in games need to make sounds for all these activities. Battles call for team shouts of warning, urgent commands, battle cries, and victory celebrations. Zombies and monsters have their own special sets of sounds, whether fighting with players, raging in a horde, or idling around sniffing for human scents.

This is an area where a voice director can provide the greatest help—or do the greatest harm. Since the advent of voice acting in games, almost every actor who has performed in one has a story of vocal stress and damage from the demands of this type of vocal work. The willingness of actors to go the extra mile, combined with the need for sound designers to get buckets of authentic, scary, and blood-curdling screams into the game, creates a perfect environment for abuse. Yet another reason why voice directors for games need to understand how the voice works and how to help actors maintain their vocal health during recording sessions. In recent years, there has been a consistent call for more attention to be paid to avoiding damaging actors' voices. Government organizations and actors' unions promoting workplace safety have put guidelines and restrictions into place, but without strong enforcement, damage still occurs.

What are the key qualities that make these sounds authentic and true? Though most all of these are "sounds," they are still acted. While they can be used in any number of situations, they will sound more authentic if they are specific—that is, if there is some imaginary PTA attached. An important distinction: Efforts should not be an illustration of circumstances. Instead, they should be a response from the body due to effort.

*Efforts*

Here's a quick rundown of a standard effort set:

1. **Breathing at Rest**. For breath to register as a sound, it will require some friction or even a slight bit of voice to register. A slight narrowing or pinching in the palate or back of the throat (as in the yogic breathing called "ujjayi") often gives enough sound to register. The lips may be open or closed for variation. Often this breath is used as an idle, a moment of standing still. This breath may also be broken up into separate inhalations and exhalations, in order for sound designers to place the exact number of breaths.
2. **Walking Breath**. A slightly faster and more labored breath, but still easy. The rhythm of this breath should not exactly mimic walking. No one breathes on every step. The attitude should be business-like and slightly determined. "As if you are on your way to the store. As if you are walking carefully, watching out for enemies."
3. **Fast Walk**. Brisk in and out breath, alternating between nose and mouth for variation (but not in a strict rhythm, or it will sound mechanistic). "As if you are just in time for a plane and walking briskly to the gate."
4. **Easy Run**. A simple jogger's breath, a breath that maintains a pace without too much strain.
5. **Medium Run**. A more labored and focused run, but not panicking.
6. **Full Out Run**. A run for your life, a run to save a comrade, a run to escape enemy attack. Can be panicked or focused, brave, and sturdy.
7. **Slowing Down/Transition Breath**. Three or four breaths to transition between a full run and walking. Should be short.
8. **Jumps and Landings**. These are normally more effective when done together. A small jump is jumping off a stool or ladder and landing on the ground. A large jump would be a superhuman feat of jumping off a ledge and making a hard landing on a nearby roof.
9. **Squeezes and Crawls**. Many games have very narrow spaces that a player must squeeze through or small areas that a player has to crawl around.

10. **Pushes and Pulls**. These are often small, medium and large. Don't be afraid to make the smallest of these very subtle. Sometimes, a sound designer needs a tiny grunt as a character picks up a tool. At the other end, a full-on groan might be needed for an ancient stuck lever. Use imaginary prompts for these: "You have to get under a house and lift if off its foundation." Or give the actor a direction like, "Try it as if, without words, your sound is commanding that stuck lever, 'Move, dammit!'"
11. **Small Damage**. These are hurts or wounds inflicted on a character. For damage, I encourage actors to utilize a "glottal onset." The breath is gathered and then released all at once. Think of a monkey's "ooh ooh" or the English, "uh oh." For the smallest wounds, I often use the image of a paper cut, or the prompt, "like walking on sharp stones in bare feet." Again here, feel confident with very small sounds. As with a paper cut, sometimes there's a hint of emotion at having so stupidly injured yourself.
12. **Medium Damage**. This hurts a bit more. A muscular pain that hurts more than you expected it to. Use parts of the body to vary the sound. A punch in the arm feels different than a punch in the thigh or a punch in the gut. There is an automatic sound that escapes the victim when taking damage. Try to evoke these responses. With damage, there is usually a slight element of surprise. No one really expects to get hit. The subtextual "Oh no you didn't!" or "WTF!" or just plain "Hey!" are good responses to suggest (as sounds, never words).
13. **Heavy Damage**. These are usually staggering amounts of pain and may be drawn out for a second or two or even three. Think of broken bone pain, a stabbing, a crushed toe with a sledge hammer. Is the sound an attempt to contain the pain, or is it a rage-fueled cry of protest? Does it leave the victim staggering or even nauseous? Experiment with different vowels for variations on damage as well.
14. **Small Attacks**. This is when the character is attempting to inflict damage on another. Attacks feel authentic to me when they come from the front of the mouth and feel focused and intentional. I often use the phrase "through gritted teeth"

to describe this "frontal" quality. Small attacks might be a lightning-quick punch, a slap, or poking someone with a pin. Remember not to illustrate the sound of the attack but to make the sound of the effort escaping from the body.

15. **Medium Attacks**. These can be thrown punches, kicks, or stabbings. There is some weight to the attack. There may be actors who have never thrown a punch, but almost everyone has swatted a bug or hammered in a nail. Pushing someone away is a good prompt for this. The voice director might throw some prompts to the actor to get an emotional quality going in the attack: "Push that drunk guy off you." "Fight off a disgusting, rotting zombie." "Swat the mosquito that's been biting you all night."
16. **Large Attacks**. These attacks involve more weight and duration. "Swing a heavy sword." "Smash a chair and enjoy it." "Pay someone back for hurting a loved one." These kinds of prompts give an emotional connection to the inflictor of the damage and power the sound with satisfying authenticity.

*Deaths*

These can really kill a voice (pun intended). The length and intensity of a game death usually has to do with the importance of a character. For a player character that will respawn, a death is usually a short, one to three second grunt or cry of pain with a tail that has a slightly breathy expiration. It needs to convey to the player, "Your character has died." These should not be too gruesome, as all players know they can never really die. They will just be sent back to an earlier checkpoint on the game. Short deaths are usually a solid and brave scream or cry that do not trail off for very long, if at all. Sound designers don't like deaths to have too many pieces to them, like a rock skipping across a pond. A solid fat waveform of sound is preferable. For bigger deaths, good variations can be found by offering subtextual prompts or even actions for death screams. (*Warning: these prompts may be triggering.*)

- **Actions**. To warn nearby comrades that the enemy is here. To get someone to rescue you. To show them they can kill your body but will never crush your spirit.

- **Emotional Moments.** You will never see your loved ones again. This death represents a failure on your part. You welcome the release from this world of suffering. An uncontrollable scream of horror escapes your lips when you see your own body cut open.
- **Body Sensations.** You've been stabbed in x, y, or z part of your body. You are set on fire and burning. You've had a red-hot piece of metal shoved into you. You are being pulled in two. You are being crushed from your feet toward your head.

*Taunts*

Taunts are "fight me" lines for both major and minor boss battles. I love "to taunt" as a verb because it is so enjoyably playable and contains great sub-actions. "To make them feel small. To goad them into fighting you. To set them up for failure. To destroy their confidence. To make them madder so they lose control."

Taunts have a lot to do with proximity to the opponent, the environment, and the previous moment. Is this a "Get out of my way and let me through" battle? Is it an ennobled "You're going to get what you deserve?" or is it a delicious "I can't wait to kick your ass" kind of fight? Have these characters fought before?

Battle taunts often have a number of variants that play depending on how the fight is going. Is the character energized and raring to go, or have they been fighting for a while and taking damage? Often, there is an, "Ok, you're better than I thought, but now I'm really going to ground myself and pull out all the stops on you." There can be the "last ditch" taunts before being beaten, or the "I've basically beaten you. Why don't you just surrender" taunts for a victory lap.

*Barks*

Barks comprise a great deal of the soundscape in many types of games. They are short, snappy battle shouts between team members, usually over gunfire or explosions. For multiplayer games, they can keep players informed of who is winning, who has the target, or who is retreating. They can be life or death reminders on the battlefield, commands, or calls for help.

Not all barks are loud. They can be short, urgent quips with others in the same room. They can also be over the radio. It's important to know the difference because the tone is quite different for each. Same room barks need clear articulation, especially since they are fast. Radio barks are very short and use minimal words.

Loud, outdoor barks really need careful pacing to avoid damage to the actor's voice. The sustained quality of many medium-loud barks can be just as damaging as death screams. On a technical note, I always encourage actors to use a "belt" quality for sustained loud barks. By extending the vowels slightly and making room in either the thyroid or cricoid cartilage in the throat, the "sound" of calling out is approximated without damage. Imagine you are at a loud nightclub, and you say to a friend, "Do you want to step outside and get some air?" The quality of your voice would be as if you were talking carefully over loud sound in order to be heard. It's easy to approximate that sound, and it isn't necessary to use a lot of air to do so. I do an exercise in my warmup where we breath out, hold, and then shout "applejacks!" There is still enough air to make the sound, but there's no chance to overload the vocal folds with too much pressure. For a longer phrase, the opposite can also work. Take a sip of air in, hold, then without taking in any more air, shout.

Give actors plenty of rest and keep them well hydrated. If you start to hear the sound thickening or dropping in pitch it means your actor's instrument is taking damage. There are solid techniques to repair a tired voice, such as straw phonation, high-pitched humming, and more. Pace very carefully and consider saving any remaining barks for the next session. Live to die another day.

### Setting the Tone

Voice recording for games can be tremendous fun. Keep the atmosphere light and creative. Remember that the booth is your office and your actors' office. No one wants to come in to a tense office where they have to produce results from the moment they arrive until the bell rings at the end of the day. The recording booth is not a fun factory. There is a flow to the day, and each actor has a different way of working and different needs. Stay present with each one and help them do their best work. By having regular and clear communication with your developers, you can be already on the same page before the session begins.

As a voice director, take care of your own mental and physical health outside of the sound studio. Share your stories and your soul with your actors and your developers. The director sets the tone for the working environment, and if you expect your actors to give 100%, and to be emotionally available, you must set the tone so that work can happen.

Give yourself something personal to work on every day, so you stay fresh. Sometimes, I come in with what I call a "basket of ideas." I research themes related to the game and pick out actions that anyone dealing with those themes might want to pursue. I keep my communication clear or make requests of co-workers. I lay down on my back during the lunch break, or stretch out and breathe between sessions. Even just remembering to thank my actors, my developers, and especially my engineer at the end of the day can freshen up my purpose. As a voice director, you are a leader, a coach, and a caretaker. It is a privilege to be assigned to do this work. Never lose sight of that, and you will have a great career.

## References

Knight, Dudley. *Speaking with Skill: An Introduction to Knight-Thompson Speechwork*. Bloomsbury Publishing Plc., 2012.

Linklater, Kristin. *Linklater Voice Work*. Kristin Linklater Voice Centre Ltd., 2024.

Rodenburg, Patsy. *The Actor Speaks: Voice and the Performer*. St. Martin's Griffin, 2002.

Shewell, Christina. *Voice Work: Art and Science in Changing Voices*. Wiley-Blackwell, 2010.

Steinhauer, Kimberly, Mary McDonald Klimek, and Jo Estill. *The Estill Voice Model: Theory & Translation*. Estill Voice International, LLC, 2017.

# 11

# Surviving and Thriving as a Videogame Performance Director

**In This Chapter**

- Establishing yourself as a director
- The importance of self-care for directors
- Dealing with reviews and online criticism
- An attitude of service
- Setting boundaries

## Establishing Yourself as a Director

Directors and actors are always asking me, "How do I get into the video game business?" I only have one answer for that: You get into it the same way you've gotten into anything else. If each of us were to trace all the things that got us to wherever we are today, chances are good that we'd see a combination of skill, training, interviewing, perseverance, networking, hard work, and plain old luck. There is no one path into the profession. Actors audition endlessly for roles, some of which they will get and many that they won't. Directors have to rely much more on networking, skill, and luck to find professional opportunities.

The Stoic philosopher Seneca said, "Luck is when preparation meets opportunity." The preparation for a career in directing is multi-faceted. Directing is a skill that calls its practitioners to be visionaries, technicians, psychologists, and negotiators. Performance directing, in particular, requires a consummate sensitivity to the emotional states of actors and the complexities of group dynamics.

 DOI: 10.1201/9781003558910-12

are loving every second of it. In such conditions, it's easy to lose sight of that love. You must give yourself the chance to replenish your energy.

A creative artist needs to put as much time into replenishment as they do into creating. Energy is like a bank account. If you're only taking funds out without putting any in, you'll run out in no time. I used to think that it was indulgent to spend too much time replenishing. It was only after I crashed and burned a few times that I learned that the replenishment rule is non-negotiable.

Years ago, I was working on a challenging project that I'd poured my heart and soul into. During the day, I was directing in the mocap volume; at night I was directing VO sessions with actors in Australia from my home in Los Angeles. One of the voice talents in Australia was a musician who had never spoken or sang in performance. But lines had been written for this person as if they were a radio DJ. Not only was the talent unused to speaking, he was also not at all facile with reading out loud. We had two nighttime sessions scheduled. After the first, it was clear that he'd never get through the material. On the second, after my day in the volume, instead of eating dinner or resting, I rewrote the entire script for the DJ. The good news is that we got through the material. The bad news was that I was so wired that I couldn't sleep. Right after that, I had to fly off to an overseas mocap shoot on a new project. It was a nine-hour time change, and to make matters worse, I still hadn't recovered from the last project. Once I landed, I was so jet lagged I could barely function.

While I was still overseas, the previous project—the one I'd poured my whole soul into—came out. The reviews were scathingly bad. I was devastated. If my work was as poor as reviews said, what was the point of continuing? I was now alone in a foreign city, in a fancy hotel room that had a balcony. For a few moments, I actually considered how easy it would be to tilt myself over the railing and be out of pain forever. Fortunately, I called a friend instead.

### Dealing with Criticism and Soliciting Feedback

I find bad reviews and negative comments to be soul crushing. It's nice when they are good, but there's no way they will all be good. Even if reviews on my projects are outstanding, if there is one snarky comment, that's all I remember. It's just the way I'm wired. I know people who like to see what is being said and claim to have such a thick skin that it doesn't affect them. But I've seen the damage that paying too much attention to critics and comments can do. It's called error-correction-error: Someone has an opinion that a director's choices are wrong. The director reads this opinion and stores it away. That's the "error" part. The next project they do, the creator does all they can to "correct" this error, making more errors based on someone's formerly limited opinion. Gradually over time, the choices creators make based on avoiding criticism put them in a smaller and smaller box, until they no longer see the point in making anything or taking a risk because inevitably it will be shot down by someone. This is a creative decay spiral. And because it's difficult to control the critics, we as creators have no choice but to work on ourselves—not on what the critics say, but on our internal ability to ignore it, process it, or set it aside.

It is our duty as artists to keep taking chances and putting out the work we believe in. This kind of risk-taking requires some insulation from random uninformed criticism. I no longer pay much attention to reviews, and I no longer let them define my career. It's part of what I call "being a grownup" to always remember that no matter what I create and put out into the world, there will always be someone who will not like it.

Publicity can be fun (sometimes) and maddening (often), but it is a reality (always). It's an important part of the marketing of our projects. Reviews belong to the publicity machine. The Oscar-winning actor Cate Blanchett said, "After the thing is made, it can be politicized, disseminated, discussed, people can be disgusted with it, offended by it, inspired by it. But that is outside our control." The great filmmaker Billy Wilder made some 50 movies but only five are really remembered. It's particularly hard to predict how a game will turn out and be received, since it takes so many people and teams to produce it.

Outside of reviews, directors need a good, reliable source for feedback. The key to getting good feedback is asking the right kinds of questions. Instead of "Did you like it?" which is entirely subjective, ask targeted questions to gauge the effectiveness and impact of your work. One developer I work with has a policy that all feedback must be "actionable." Good questions for getting feedback are things like, "How did the scene make you feel?" "Who drew your attention most in the scene?" "Was there any moment when you weren't interested?" "Did you understand what the scene was about?" "What questions came up in your mind while you were watching the scene?" Test your theories about subtext, emotional moments, or turning points by asking observers targeted questions. You will get much more out of feedback if you do. If you do get *I-liked-it-I-didn't-like-it*-type comments, probe deeper.

Game developers often lack the vocabulary to give actionable feedback on dramatic scenes. I was once asked to re-cast an actor who had two major pcap scenes that book-ended a level in the game; he also had voice-over narration throughout the level. And he'd already done the work. Suffice to say, I was pretty invested in keeping this actor—he was an excellent choice for the role and I had directed his stellar performance throughout. Executives said, "He's not good." This feedback came down through a chain of command that I didn't have access to, so I asked to review a playback of the level.

Watching it, I saw the problem right away. As so often happens, there was a disconnect between what we imagined in the booth and what was on the screen. The narration was taking the player out of the experience instead of framing it. I asked for one more session with the actor to re-record the entire level to picture. The results made a huge difference, and the actor's work stayed in the game, to much acclaim. **ADR dubbing** can make a big difference in a performance. One or two tweaks to a line here or there can make an awkward or lackluster performance shine. Unfortunately, the production process can hamper this level of attention. When the crunch comes, developers lose sight of the many small nuances that add up to the success or failure of a scene. Often, the fixes are easy, but due to budgetary and time constrains, easy fixes get passed over and the narrative aspects of a game fall apart. It doesn't have to be that way.

Quality, actionable feedback can be a source of nourishment for a director. When my developers give me notes that help me understand what they are looking for—notes that go beyond "I don't like it," I feel respected as a collaborator. I can filter them through my own creativity, my own craft, to stay true to the subtext and find engaging actions and images for myself and my actors. They are respecting my boundaries as a creative artist. It's the same when I give actors feedback or direction through action verbs or images. It respects their work and their agency to shape their own performance. When the work is flowing in this way, it's energizing.

### Setting Boundaries

Boundary-setting is part of the **replenishment chain.** Replenishing can also mean setting a boundary to *not* doing certain things, *not* participate in struggles that are not ours or not necessary. At times, being with friends or meeting with colleagues is replenishing. At other times, it's a drain on our creativity and time. We have to make conscious choices about saying yes or no to demands on our time or energy. Boundaries come in many different forms, from strict to permeable. They protect our energy, preserve our health, and keep us safe.

Boundaries also keep those around us safe. As a job-givers and decision makers, directors have an inherent power imbalance with those they direct. A director's ethics must be pristine and always within the law. That means no *quid pro quo* (Latin "this for that") with actors for assigning roles. The only thing an actor owes you in exchange for a role is to show up on time, ready to work.

Be careful about accepting gifts from actors. A small token of thanks or appreciation is fine, but expensive gifts move dangerously close to bribery. Pristine ethics also dictate a clear boundary against an intimate relationship between a director and an actor with whom they are currently working. Attractions between people working closely together are normal, but acting on them during the work period is risky because of the very nature of the power imbalance. Only by knowing ourselves and our sensitivities, and keeping clear boundaries, can we successfully negotiate the wins and losses in the sphere of public opinion.

Balancing work and personal life are very important for a director. It can be highly addicting to be in the director's chair day after day with everyone looking to you as a leader. Make sure you spend time away from work. Take in other forms of creativity besides acting-based storytelling. Visit museums, listen to music, read books. Spend time with others. Take care of pets and walk in nature. Give back to the community through service. Walk through a city where no one knows you or what you do for a living. If you need to justify time away from work, remember that in order to tell stories that feel alive and emotionally resonant, you must never lose touch with everyday life.

### The Challenge (and Benefits) of Serving Others

In the many years I've been in this business, perhaps the greatest truth is that I'm not alone in this endeavor. That means not only do I have the support of others and their talents, but also that I am here to serve them. Even doing your own material as a producer/writer/director/editor/actor, you will need to adopt an attitude of service. Particularly in videogames, where collaboration is king and queen, you, dear reader, will be answering to someone. Someone will have a vision, someone will have the budget, someone will need to sign off, someone will be evaluating, and ultimately the game-players will decide if your story or performance is compelling. Compound that with the fact that the story you write, shoot, or record may be edited and put into a context decided by somebody else. Welcome to the business. But oddly enough, all of this service can resolve into an empowering and creatively fulfilling career.

Performance directing in collaboration with stakeholders requires a flexible, dynamic leadership style. You must take in the needs and desires of all the collaborators and run them through the mill of your own vision. If your idea is that you will become an auteur, an *enfant terrible* whose unique vision will be made manifest, you should probably pick a medium other than games, most likely one you can self-finance.

I actually *enjoy* the fact that producing games takes teams and teams of creative minds working together toward a goal. Sometimes, it works better than others, but the process is invigorating and generally the team adds up to more than the sum of its parts. The storytelling in most games is so complex that no one person can entirely dictate the outcome. You can barely make a decision on the set that doesn't require a message back to home base to see if the design teams can handle a change.

*Move a sofa?* We can do it. *Add a small table?* Can't happen. *Tie something in a bundle?* Sure, as long as you hide it from the camera, otherwise it would take too much hand animation to show properly. *Can she touch her hair?* She can touch it, but the hair can't move. *Wipe the bar with a cloth?* OK, but it has to be a stiff cloth. He can't squeeze it or bunch it.

I once had an actor come on set to do an intense scene where he is preparing for a suicide mission as revenge for the killing of his fiancé. He's lying on his bunk, and a few other characters come to discuss plans with him. The actor had prepared the scene well, but unfortunately, he based his preparation on holding a picture of the dead fiancé and a piece of her clothing. I had to inform him that this was impossible. He didn't take it well. But the fact was that the prop department had not created a 3-D object that could be a picture, and costumes did not have a budget to add a digital piece of clothing. Plus, due to limitations of the headcam technology recording his facial movements, the actor couldn't touch his face or rub his eyes while the cameras were rolling.

But the actor found it impossible to access the necessary emotional state in the scene without these props and a bunch of grief-stricken hand-gestures to his face. It really takes a flexible actor with a good imagination to play in this medium. And you as a director are responsible for making sure the actor's demands fit with the necessary parameters of the project. Any choice you make can create extra work for animators and scenic artists who already have a budgeted time and scope.

### Tales from the Working Life

*Letting Go of Ego*

In the summer of 2016, I received an urgent message from a producer asking if I was available to direct a last-minute performance-capture project. As with all videogames, the security around the content was very tight, but it was teased to me that this was a very high-level project. A real "career-making opportunity." The cast had already been selected and booked, but for some reason there was no director attached.

As soon as the NDA (non-disclosure agreement) was signed I was told that the project was for a major franchise. A dream project had fallen into my lap! With very little time to prepare, I threw myself into directing prep for the vertical slice (a small test piece of the game).

I read and re-read the script, identified themes, came up with lists of questions, and researched the source material by watching movies associated with this franchise.

The shoot was very much on the fly. The actors were solid but not exactly right for the roles, the cinematographer was there merely to record video, and the script was a work in progress. The development team was open to all of my suggestions and at the end seemed quite pleased with the performances. There was eager talk of continuing the work in the fall.

A few months passed and there was no word. I was having lunch with a friend who knew the producer, and I asked if they had heard anything about the project. He was taken aback. "Oh, you directed that?" He gave me a strange look and changed the subject. I knew something had happened.

I phoned the producer, who told me that I would not be directing the project after all. There was a new creative director coming on board and they would be selecting the performance director themself. However, since I had some familiarity with the project, would I be available to help with the casting? Perhaps direct the auditions?

I asked the producer to give me a day to think it over. An old feeling of humiliation and shame crept over me. I should have known better than to dive in to a project that didn't even have a director a week before the shoot. Was I so hungry for success that I would say yes without thoroughly vetting a project? Did I really bomb that bad? Was I fooling myself thinking I knew how to direct?

I had helped cast a few projects that I wasn't directing, and I really didn't like doing it. Casting is very, very important and takes people who are knowledgeable, talented and dedicated. As a director, however, my heart wasn't in it. I felt like I was planning someone else's wedding when I really wanted to get married myself. I decided to turn the job down.

But a small voice inside me told me to reconsider: *Give up your ego and stay involved with the project. This project is yours.* I had an unshakable feeling that with the open and experimental nature of auditions, I could explore some interesting things with the actors, and the producers would reconsider and eventually offer me the directing job.

I was right. I ended up performance-directing *Star Wars: Battlefront II.* I was in high heaven. The script was developing into something wonderful. The cast was extraordinary, and some of the actors remain close friends today. But that was not the final turn of events for this game.

Around launch, the reviews for the acting were very good, but an intractable problem reared its head. *Loot Boxes.* Loot boxes, which the developers had included in the game-play, were part of a growing trend of providing players with opportunities to make in-app purchases. A player could purchase a loot box within the game that could have any number of potential upgrades. The rub was that they didn't know what was in the box. It was, to use the operative and dangerous word, a gamble. Players disliked it immediately, calling it *pay-to-win.* To make matters worse, several European governments considered banning the game. The developers removed the boxes, and the game eventually found its footing. But the damage was done.

I went on to direct two more *Star Wars* games, both of which were highly successful. But the difficult *Battlefront II* experience taught me something profound on many levels. Always listen to your intuition, even if it means swallowing your pride. And never depend on the outcome of a project. It's out of your control.

### *The Vampire's Voice*

Sometimes, the somebodies you have to serve are larger corporate interests. When my original games employer was acquired by the French company Vivendi, they also acquired Universal Studios. Suddenly, we were doing games based on motion pictures put out by Universal. One such game was *Van Helsing,* a big effects-based horror show starring Hugh Jackman, directed by Stephen Sommers of *The Mummy* fame. Having worked at Universal previously, in their animation department, I knew that horror was a staple for Universal and the studio had the rights to many classic characters.

I was assigned to cast and direct the voice-over for the game based on the movie. For casting, I was given a few lines of copy from the game, and a one-line sample of each character's voice performance.

When I inquired whether it was possible to get the original actors to do the voices, I was told, "Maybe."

Meanwhile, the company tasked me with finding voice matches for every character. I kept pressing for an opportunity to at least go after Hugh Jackman. The executive producer finally relented but gave me such a ridiculously small budget that I knew Jackman's people would never agree. Still, we made the offer, and were rebuffed. A small, robust cast of solid voice actors were assembled and approved. Recording began off a spreadsheet of voice lines. On the first day, sitting next to the producer who I was depending on for my life (since the spreadsheet contained little-to-no information about the context of the lines), I noticed he seemed to be referring to a document when he didn't know the answers off hand.

"What's that?" I politely inquired.

"Oh, the script."

*What????* "Um, do you think I could have one of those?" I assumed he could read the dripping sarcasm in my voice.

"Sorry, it's all confidential. I'll have to see if I can get approval for that."

Since the thousands of lines in a game are assembled in spreadsheets, it's tragically too often that a spreadsheet is all that's given to directors and actors. Deciphering these spreadsheets to understand context is a frustrating treasure hunt. Still, you have to do your best, you have to serve somebody, and assume these little oversights—like not sharing the script with the director—are honest mistakes made by well-meaning people.

But things were about to get worse.

A few weeks after the script was fully recorded, I was summoned to the office of the executive producer. "What's this?" he demanded. "This recording is terrible! These performances sound nothing like the original actors!"

I tactfully reminded him that all we had to go on in casting was one line from each character, and that I'd tried to get the original actors, and that he himself had given me a ridiculously small amount of money for Jackman. This did nothing to appease him.

"Can you prove this?" he demanded. "Can you prove you reached out to him and he turned it down?"

All the paper trails in the world won't get you out of trouble when someone wants to make you the scapegoat. The Powers That Be decided that procuring the movie actors had to be taken into bigger hands than those of small fry like me. Negotiations ensued, and weeks later I found myself in New York City, where Hugh Jackman was starring on Broadway in *The Boy From Oz*. Hugh was booked to record with me for the next two days, along with a few other members of the cast, including Schuler Hensley, who played Frankenstein. Hugh was amazing in *The Boy From Oz*, completely present, a consummate musical theater performer in this story of a gay singer-songwriter from Australia who rose to fame and then, at the height of his career, died tragically from AIDS. Jackman was the same in the studio, wonderfully available, curious, open to my direction.

Back in LA, the Powers That Be were having trouble. The *Van Helsing* film was finishing post-production, but the game producers were having trouble closing deals with the rest of the cast, who were all in town for ADR voice recording for the film. I was given a hard drive and instructed to drive to the Fox lot where a parking pass would be waiting: I was to go to the sound stage where the sound was recording, wait around until I was given the signal, and "try to get the rest of the cast to record."

This, you'll understand, was an anxious moment. In those days, videogames were (and still are in some quarters) something no one wanted to bother with, something equal to kids' toys that somehow got rolled into an actor's overall deal. Top actors looked at games as more work for no extra pay. This was 2003. The horrors of September 11, 2001, were still fresh, and security at the studio was high. I waited at the gates as security scanned the underside of my car with a mirror. The seconds seemed to be moving very, very slowly. I considered my options: I could run screaming from the lot. I could walk in, wander around, and claim later that I couldn't find the room. Or I could suck it up and move forward.

The one thing I had going for me was the thick orange hard drive sitting next to me in the passenger seat. It represented the power of the game studio and my position as the representative of that studio. I decided to move forward. My entire professional life, it seemed, was on the line. I was walking through a wall of fire; my ego was being burned off. Somehow, I knew that if I got what I came for, whatever was left of me would be stronger, more solid, and more assured.

My moment had come. I poked my head in the door.

Some sound engineer stopped me right there.

"Wait out in the corridor."

OK, my moment hadn't come. Yet. I found a vending machine. To this day, I can taste the cheesy crackers and cola I used to shove down my feelings.

Finally, they let me in to get the lines I needed from the first actor, who was understandably short-tempered. He couldn't grasp the concept that in a game, the character might be at a different proximity from the player at different moments, and that I needed two levels of projection for each line, one for close and one for distance. The entire time, executives from the film were lounging on a couch behind me, making fun of me. I think I asked them to keep it down, but I can't be sure.

Somehow, I persevered and left with a full hard drive.

I certainly learned something from that experience. By facing my fears and walking through my own "wall of fire," I never again felt "less than" in any professional situation. It's odd that from my current vantage point, 20 years later, videogames are on par with or outselling movies as a form of popular entertainment.

An attitude of service can be a north star for any director. Vision is important, but a vision must be pressed into service of the moment. As soon as a project is born, it takes on a life of its own. A parent can have a vision for their child, but if the vision doesn't serve the child and the other stakeholders in the child's life, there will be nothing but misery and failure. As a leader, you must serve the circumstances of the moment. Like a boxer, you have to bob and weave and adjust to what the world is giving you. As the Stoics say, the obstacle is the way. Wise adjustment is the path to creative triumph.

## References

Blanchett, Cate. Venice Film Festival. Venice, Italy, 2022.

Holiday, Ryan, and Stephen Hanselman. *The Daily Stoic: 366 Meditations on Wisdom, Perseverance, and the Art of Living.* Penguin Random House, 2016.

*Star Wars Battlefront II*. Developed by Electronic Arts, DICE, Motive Studios, and Criterion Games, Electronic Arts, 2017.

The Boy from Oz. Directed by Philip Wm. McKinley, performances by Hugh Jackman, Isabel Keating, and Jarrod Emick, Imperial Theatre, Broadway, 2003–2004.

*Van Helsing*. Directed by Stephen Sommers, performances by Hugh Jackman, Kate Beckinsale, and Richard Roxburgh, Universal Pictures, 2004.

Weston, Judith. *The Film Director's Intuition: Script Analysis and Rehearsal*. Michael Wiese Productions, 2003.

Weston, Judith. *Directing Actors: Creating Memorable Performances for Film and Television*. Michael Wiese Productions, 2021.

# APPENDIX A
## WARMUP

I use the following as a guide for warming up the body and voice before a performance capture session, which can also be useful for theater, film or any performance setting.

**IMPORTANT: If you are leading actors through a warmup, make sure you emphasize that they should work gently, never straining. There should be no pain in these exercises. They can adapt the exercise to feel comfortable. Physical exercises can also be modified and done in a chair. Vocal exercises should never feel "scratchy" or "tight." If they do, stop immediately.**

1. **Set a simple standing stance** with legs hip-width apart, pelvis hanging toward the floor, knees slightly bent, shoulders wide and easy, head up and gently lifted.
2. **Warm up the spine.** Hang forward with knees bent or straight. Do a simple twist to right and left. Gently side bend.
3. **Open the breath** with forward hang, sending the impulse of the breath deep into the pelvis in various positions including hanging over or with elbows on knees. Try a slow roll-up from hanging. Explore a self-hug with breath across the back. Side bends can be done with attention paid to the movement of the ribs on inhale and exhale. Explore some deep "hah" sounds and sighs as if they are originating deep in the lower belly (Figure A.1).

**Figure A.1** Voice and body warmup: opening the ribs with breath. The author with actors Debra Wilson, Victoria Atkin, T.J. Ramini, and Elizabeth Grullon. (Photo by Katja Kulenkampff.)

4. **Rotate the arms and legs** gently in their sockets. Progress to an easy swinging of the arms and legs. (Use a chair or wall for balance if needed for leg swings.)
5. **Loosen and massage the jaw**. Gently stroke the jaw open and forward. Purse lips and smile wide (Kiss/smile), stick out your tongue and retract it. Lick around upper and lower teeth.
6. **Hum into the head** with "mmm" "nnn" and sensing resonance as buzz around the head. Try that on different pitches. **Warm up nasal twang** with some "nyeah nyeahs," the way children do when goading each other. **Yawn** while stretching up the right and left.
7. **Make the *ng* sound** and siren/slide up and down from resting pitch to higher and lower pitches keeping the tongue in the 'ng' sound position.
8. **"Whimper"** in your highest pitch.
9. **"Hoo"** like an owl in your highest pitch.
10. **Make very deep low-pitched sounds** in a round and open manner.

11. **Easy shout or "belt,"** without strain, call to a friend in another room. Make a big expansive "ayy" (as in "say") like the classic New York pizza guy.
12. **Light easy jog or prance** in place while warming up and rotating the fingers and wrists.
13. **Warm up your diction** with tongue twisters—I like Dr. Suess' "Fox in Sox" for good tongue twisters.
14. **Big jolly** operatic laughing or sobbing.
15. **Finish by coming together as a group** with sound and/or presence. This can be something of your own devising. You might sing one note together, focusing on making a group sound. Stand silently and invite each person to meet with their eyes. Use this moment to offer a daily guiding watchword such as "precision," "focus," or "generosity." Or dedicate the day's work to a particular theme.

## Reference

Seuss, Dr. *Fox in Socks*. Beginner Books, 1965.

# Glossary

**Action.** The physical or emotional activity given to a character in a scene. Usually expressed as a verb. "To ___." Can also be thought of as a purpose or intention.

**Actor language.** An imaginative way for directors to speak to actors, considering the training of actors and the tools actors use to bring their performances to life. Expresses as actions, images, "as ifs" etc.

**ACTRA.** Alliance of Canadian Cinema, Television and Radio Artists. Trade union representing Canadian artists.

**Acts.** Large portions of a drama or comedic piece.

**ADR dubbing.** Stands for "Automated Dialogue Replacement." Process by which actors replace or add dialogue to picture.

**ADR/walla.** Stands for "Automated Dialogue Replacement." Walla usually refers to background sounds in a game, literally the murmur of a crowd.

**Affective memory.** An exercise from Method acting that involves using sensory cues to re-experience an emotional event and create a truthful response in the actor.

**Animal exercise.** An exercise in which actors embody the physical characteristics or rhythms of an animal in portraying a character.

**Art of experiencing.** A concept from great Russian acting master Constantin Stanislavski, who argued that the art of experiencing is a preferred method for an actor to truthfully embody a role vs. the mere illustration or representation of a role.

**Art of representation.** A concept from Stanislavski, who argued that the art of representation is an outdated method of merely illustrating emotions vs. truly inhabiting the role as if living through the character.

**As if.** An acting tool that enables a performer to apply imaginary circumstance internally in order to personalize their choices for a character. "As if we were in a restaurant with candles and wine."

**Assets.** The technical name for previously created artwork needed for a motion-capture session. Involves the sets, backgrounds, props, and character dimensions necessary for accurately measuring out the spaces a performer will inhabit.

**Audio director.** Person in charge of all the audio files needed for the game, from dialogue to SFX to music.

**Battle sequences.** Segments of a game where the player engages with enemies spawned by AI in the game engine. Usually, a sonically rich environment requiring the voice actors to be speaking, shouting, or screaming at top volume and with urgency.

**Beats.** Moments in a scene where a particular topic is being discussed or an emotional energy is being exchanged.

**Blocking rehearsal.** A rehearsal where the dimensions of the spaces set up by the environment designers are marked with tape on the floor and the key moments of actors' positions are determined.

**Blocking.** The movement of actors during a scene in the volume.

**Booth.** A sound booth where the actor is isolated and records audio for the game.

**Breakdown.** Casting term for a document detailing the character descriptions and background information for auditioning actors.

**Capture.** The process of recording digital movement or sound data from actors.

**Character walk.** Style of walking that personifies a character played by an actor, different from the actor's normal way of walking. A character's way of walking reveals a lot about them and is important in motion capture.

**Choices.** An actor's internal and external ideas and cues that create their unique interpretation of a character and scenes.

**Cinematic director.** Person in charge of designing and executing the cinematics in a game.

**Cinematic.** Usually a locked "movie" in a game where the player has limited or no interactive abilities. Cinematics are set pieces that move the story along, show an event from the past, or give insight into a character's motivations.

**Circumstances.** The environment and situation characters find themselves in, which the actors must appear to be truthfully inhabiting and responding to.

**Creative director.** A member of the team developing the game who has overall responsibility for the look and feel of the experience.

**Denouement.** The final part of a narrative in which the various parts of the story come together and the conflicts in the story are resolved.

**Director's vision.** An idea or concept the performance director holds which is unforgettably compelling and interesting but flexible enough to accommodate the input of the creative team and the actors.

**Emotional event.** The moment in a scene where something important is exchanged or the dynamic of the characters shift and the stakes of the narrative are changed.

**Equity.** Trade union representing videogame actors in the UK and Canada.

**Events.** Moments that happen within and scene or outside of a scene that characters must respond to. Important for directors to identify in order to properly shape a scene.

**Facts of the scene.** Verifiable truths about the situation or characters outside of their emotional reactions or thoughts. Important for directors to identify so that their creative choices for the scene are in harmony with what the player will grasp seeing the scene for the first time.

**Five-act structure.** A traditional dramatic structure, including exposition, rising action, climax, falling action, and resolution.

**Game director.** Member of the game development team who has an executive and creative responsibility for the entire game.

**Generalized expression.** A clichéd facial or physical expression of an emotion that lacks nuance and specificity.

**Giving an adjustment.** The art of speaking to an actor about a choice they have made. An adjustment respects the actor's choice and "adjusts" it to fit in the director's vision or the truth of the scene.

**Habituation.** The tendency for an actor to revert to a choice they rehearsed or played previously, which blocks them from acting on an adjustment they've received from a director.

**Homework.** Preparatory work a director or actor does to explore the script, come up with choices, and note personal connections to the material.

**Illustrating.** Similar to the "the art of representation," the tendency of an actor to physicalize emotions without feeling them. Can also mean using the body and voice to give a generalized meaning to a word or line regardless of the intention of the line. E.g., looking up in the air and smiling while saying "it's a nice day."

**Improvisation.** Working with a scene or situation in a way that has not been planned.

**Levels.** A series of sequences in a game similar to the acts in a play or film. Levels usually involve a set location or series of challenges that are grouped together in pursuit of an objective.

**Local experience.** The author's term for looking at the activities and perspective of a character through the lens of their everyday life.

**Markers.** Reflective balls applied at the joints on a mocap suit.

**Mocap (see motion capture).** Acronym for motion capture.

**Mocap suits.** Form-fitting, Velcro-friendly suits worn by mocap actors which hold reflective markers at the joints.

**Motion capture.** Technique of capturing data from a body in motion through the use of reflective light.

**Multiplayer.** A form of gaming where multiple players compete against each other or in teams in real time.

**Obstacle.** A concept in acting whereby the actor imagines something blocking the character from directly achieving their goals.

**Open-world walk-and-talks.** Sequences in a game where characters trade dialogue while transversing through various spaces in a game.

**Pcap (see performance capture).** Acronym for performance capture.

**Performance capture.** Technique of capturing an actor's movement, sound, and facial data simultaneously.

**Performance director.** Person responsible for directing the acting in a game through voice over, motion capture, or performance capture.

**Personal object.** Acting technique evolved from Stanislavski where an actor imagines a prop to be something of personal or magical value.

**Personalization.** An actor's tool whereby they bring an immediacy and authenticity to a moment or relationship by imagining it to be about something deeply personal to themselves.

**Place.** The physical environment or circumstances where a scene is set and impact the actor's performance. The first part of Place, Time, Action.

**Playable actions.** Internal verbs that actors hold in their minds that produce a shift in the environment or another character.

**Previous moment.** The circumstances or situation which occurred before the current scene, which carry an impact on a character's choices or emotional state.

**Previs (also previz).** Short for previsualization. Can be anything from drawings, an animatic, or live action video. Used to test the timing and staging of complex visual scenes.

**Private moment.** Stanislavski-based acting exercise where an actor, in front of an audience, performs an activity without self-consciousness, as if they were completely alone.

**PTA.** Place, Time, Action. The three essential facts the director and actors must know to find the strength and subtext in a scene.

**Rehearsal.** A process by which actors and directors explore and try out staging ideas, and in the process become familiar with the dynamics of a scene before it is performed.

**Replenishment chain.** The practices of self-care directors build into their routine to restore their energy and creativity when depleted.

**Result-oriented direction.** A controlling form of feedback from a director to an actor that undercuts an actor's creativity and expression. When directors articulate the end-result they would like to see, such as saying "do it more sad" and the classic "faster, funnier, more color" they push the actor toward superficially illustrating emotions. Telling an actor how to say the lines, known as "giving line reads" is another form of result direction that is highly disempowering.

**ROMS.** Stands for range of motion, a series of movements that an actor performs before beginning a motion capture session. ROMs establish how much a particular actor's body joints or facial features typically move and help the motion capture system calibrate the actor.

**SAG-AFTRA.** Acronym for Screen Actors Guild-American Federation of Television and Radio Artists. Both are American trade unions that merged in 2012 and represent the labor interests of actors in videogames captured in the United States and union members around the world.

**Scene.** A continuous interaction between characters in a single location.

**Script notes.** Comments given by a performance director or other team members to the writers of a narrative script.

**Sense memory.** Stanislavski-based exercise where an actor recalls the sensory details of a memory in order to trigger emotion.

**Sensory choices.** Choices in which an actor may call upon internal or external sensory cues to realistically portray a character in a situation.

**Shadow.** Psychological term for the repressed parts of a personality, either negative or positive.

**Sides.** Slang term for scripts containing an actor's lines.

**Slate.** (1) The moment in an audition where an actor states their name and other casting information (such as height, location, representation). (2) A production practice where a "clapperboard" is struck at the beginning of a scene to assist audio and picture sync in post-production.

**Specificity.** Detailed choices about behavior and emotional life that assist an actor in truthfully responding.

**Spine.** Acting term for a singular verb, image, or idea that powers a character for the entire story.

**Staging.** Like blocking, the movement of actors and objects within the performing space.

**Substitution.** An actor's tool to mentally or emotionally swap a fictional situation for a personally affecting one.

**Subtext.** The life below the words and the reasons for the choices characters make that are not readily apparent.

**Subtextual idea.** A concept that ties all the disparate parts of the story together in a thematic way.

**Table read.** A structure where actors, in the presence of the director and producers, gather and read the script out loud together for the first time.

**Three-act structure.** A classic form of dramatic structure. In simple form, Act 1 sets up the conflict, Act 2 explores rising complications, and Act 3 resolves the conflict.

**(The) Method.** A style of acting developed by Lee Strasberg from the teachings of Stanislavski.

**Time.** The second pillar in Place, Time, Action. Time refers to "what just happened," "previous moment" and "why now?"

**T-pose.** The position an actor in a mocap suit takes at the beginning and end of every take. The T-pose allows the mocap system to calibrate each actor's separate dots as belonging to them before and after the scene. Also known as A-pose.

**VCam.** A virtual camera that enables a director to see actors in mocap suits, fully realized as they will appear in the game environment, by looking through the viewfinder or monitor.

**Vertical slice.** A small section of a game that tests whether a team has all the necessary ingredients and technology to make the game on time and within budget.

**VO (see Voiceover).** Acronym for voiceover.

**Voiceover.** A form of acting that only involves an actor's voice. Most of the performance aspects of videogames are in voiceover.

**Volume.** The stage where motion capture and performance capture sessions are held. Reflects the fact that the performer's data is being captured in three dimensions from all sides and angles simultaneously.

**Word repetition game.** A basic acting exercise of the Meisner Technique in which actors repeat lines back and forth to each other to tune their listening skills and free their impulses.

**Workshop.** The author's term for the process of taking a script from the written page to the booth or stage. Workshop includes team notes, table reads, blocking rehearsals, previs, and other preparatory practices.

# Index

Note: *Italic* page numbers refer to figures.